PRENTICE-HALL
FOUNDATIONS OF CATHOLIC THEOLOGY SERIES

FOUNDATIONS OF CATHOLIC THEOLOGY SERIES

Gerard S. Sloyan, *Editor*

THE CHURCH
OF CHRIST

MAURICE BONAVENTURE SCHEPERS, OP

The Catholic University of America
Washington, D.C.

PRENTICE-HALL, INC.
Englewood Cliffs, N.J.

Imprimi potest:

William D. Marrin, OP
Provincial, Province of St. Joseph

Nihil obstat:

Kevin Seasoltz, OSB
Censor Deputatus

Imprimatur:

✠ Patrick A. O'Boyle, DD
Archbishop of Washington
February 14, 1963

The *nihil obstat* and *imprimatur* are official declarations that a book or pamphlet is free of doctrinal or moral error. No implication is contained therein that those who have granted the *nihil obstat* and *imprimatur* agree with the content, opinions, or statements expressed.

PRENTICE-HALL INTERNATIONAL, INC., *London*
PRENTICE-HALL OF AUSTRALIA, PTY., LTD., *Sydney*
PRENTICE-HALL OF CANADA, LTD., *Toronto*
PRENTICE-HALL FRANCE, S.A.R.L., *Paris*
PRENTICE-HALL OF JAPAN, INC., *Tokyo*
PRENTICE-HALL DE MEXICO, S.A., *Mexico City*

Photos: Details from the tympanum over the door of the church of La Madeleine, Vezelay, France. Courtesy Marburg—Art Reference Bureau.

C

EDITOR'S NOTE

This series offers the depth and richness of the divine message of salvation proclaimed to us by Christ. The theology, or "faith seeking understanding," contained here is not on a catechetical level, nor yet on a complex, higher level; it is clear and nontechnical, but at the same time adult and thorough. It is a scholarly presentation of revelation.

These volumes do not adopt an apologetic approach. They

neither attempt to justify Catholic faith nor aim at convincing those who do not profess it of the reasonableness of believing. This series is written primarily for those who already believe, who accept the Church as the living continuation of Christ, and the Scriptures as divinely inspired.

The authors do not attempt a philosophy of God or of Christianity, but a study of the mystery of God seen through the eyes of faith. The mystery of faith will not be dispelled by the study of these books. It will remain.

Since some background in philosophy on the part of the reader is needed, and cannot in every case be presumed, there are times when philosophical terms will need to be explained. Philosophical reasoning is very much a part of speculative theology.

Although the breakdown of the series is along traditional lines, each volume is designed to emphasize the oneness of God's plan of salvation and not its different facets. Distinction is made in order to unite. What is taught in the Scriptures is stressed, so that it may be seen how men of the Bible understood the message entrusted to them. The historical aspects of doctrine as held by Christians are then treated: the testimony of the early Christian writers and the liturgy to the belief of the Church; the controversies and heresies that necessitated defense and precise formulation, and finally, the magisterial teaching in each subject area. In this way speculative theology, or the present understanding of each mystery, is not seen in isolation from the sources of faith.

Thus, the revealed Christian message is viewed as the *tradition* (in the fullest and best sense of that theological term) expressed in and through the Church over the centuries—more explicitly formulated, from age to age, and with further applications. But it is still the same saving message begun in the Old Testament and perfected in the mystery and person of Jesus Christ.

One last point is important. Although the study of theology is an exercise of intellect, it can never be exclusively this. The message of Jesus Christ is a living Word, an invitation to participate in the saving event of the redemption, starting in this world by faith and the union of grace, and culminating in heaven by vision and immediate union. This invitation demands response or living faith. The study of the Christian message through theology requires such response, for the message is not something that was heard and assented to once. It is a Word addressed to us that requires our vigorous "Yes" for a lifetime.

CONTENTS

CHAPTER SEVEN

Holiness of the Church through the power of order. The juridical mission of the Church.

PART TWO—THE LOVE OF GOD
AND THE ACTION OF THE CHURCH

CHAPTER EIGHT

Homogeneity of the Church Militant and the Church Triumphant. The hierarchy of the new Jerusalem.

CHAPTER NINE

Activity proper to the Church. The Church's activity in the temporal order.

INTRODUCTION

St. Thomas Aquinas would have been the last person in the
world to identify his synthetic approach to divine mysteries,
conceived and executed in the *Summa Theologiae,* with theology. His intention was not to say the last word on any given
problem but to introduce young students to the wisdom of
theology, thereby helping them to become more sensitive to
the mysteries of faith. St. Thomas' rationale is one that is

valid today. Acquiring something of the wisdom of theology, he believed, is the lifetime, even if not the fulltime, job of those Christians equipped to comprehend it.

The most basic relation of this little volume to the intention of the Angelic Doctor is a negative one, for St. Thomas seemed convinced that he ought not to be writing an ecclesiology—a theology of the Church. Nearly one hundred years before his lifetime, when the movement of scholasticism had just begun, another Catholic theologian had proposed that a like venture should have as its framework the mystery of the Church. Robert of Melun (d. 1167), had proposed that the mystery of "the whole Christ, head and members," be established as the subject of theology. St. Thomas refused to accept this view, observing that "This science does treat of such things, but always in relation to God." (Cf. *S.Th.*, 1ª,1,7)

To conclude from these considerations, however, that St. Thomas is not a *magister* of the mystery of the Church would not be correct. The master idea of his synthetic approach to the mystery of God can very profitably be grafted onto the theology of the Church. This idea, moreover, is stated germinally in his rejection of Robert of Melun's proposal: ". . . *always* in relation to God." This means that the study of theology must be altogether theocentric.

All other subjects that the theologian can consider, especially the subject of man, must be considered in relation to God, that is, either as *proceeding from* him, the Alpha, as creature from Creator, or as *returning to* him, the Omega of all things. This is the plan that M.-D. Chenu has labelled *"exitus-reditus."* Understanding its meaning gives us a valuable insight into the order which St. Thomas saw as integral to the *Summa Theologiae.*

A good paraphrase of this idea in connection with the theology of the Church would run somewhat as follows: *This part of the science of theology touches many things, but they are always treated in relation to Christ.* In this statement is implied the analogy according to which the order of this brief study is conceived. The Church belongs to Christ. She depends on him. She is his creation, and as such proceeds from him and returns to him. All of this is verified in a manner comparable to the dependence of the entire universe upon God. The Church is the new creation (cf. 2 Cor 5,17); it is in terms of this Pauline figure that we shall study the mystery.

2

This brief treatment will not be, therefore, an apology of the Church of Christ. Its purpose is neither to present proofs that there exists a Church of Christ, nor to demonstrate that the Roman Catholic Church is truly that Church. Supposing these things to be true, we are attempting, instead, to present the elements of this mystery in a way that will enable the student to penetrate its meaning and discern the relation among the various aspects of the mystery.

Two things going on today that make our age a privileged one are the biblical renewal and the liturgical revival. Certainly these manifestations of vigor in Catholic life are *of the Church*: they are either "ecclesial" or they are sterile. It is not too far-fetched to say that a good theology of the Church is the best means toward understanding both why it is necessary to read the Bible intelligently, and the great importance worship has in the lives of Christian people. In the Bible the mystery of the Church is presented in figures which have ecclesiological principles as their meanings, insofar as they are understood according to the "analogy of faith" and the *sensus Ecclesiae*. Liturgical worship is, moreover, the living manifestation of the mystery of the Church. In it there are present, at least virtually, the main elements of the mystery.

Those who use this volume are reminded that it is meant to be a manual, that is, only an aid or guide in preparing the student for his own understanding of the mystery of the Church.

PART ONE

THE WISDOM
OF GOD AND
THE CONSTITUTION
OF THE CHURCH

The Church is holy
Her life depends on Christ, in whom is the fulness of grace and truth.

CHAPTER ONE

CHRIST AND HIS CHURCH

WISDOM, GRACE, TRUTH INCARNATE

At the beginning of St. John's gospel, in a passage which the priest reads as his departure prayer at the end of the Mass in several rites, the evangelist presents a panorama of God's plan to communicate his life to man. He goes back to the origin of all things, somewhat in the manner of the author of the opening part of Genesis in telling the story of creation. In this case however St. John, after beginning in the reaches of eternity, in which the "Word was with God," arrives quickly at a point in history which St. Paul calls the "fullness of time" (Gal 4,4): "And the Word was made flesh, and dwelt among us. And we saw his glory—glory as of the only-begotten of the Father—full of grace and of truth." (Jn 1,14)

The plenitude of supernatural gifts which accrue to the human nature of Jesus Christ—the object of special study in the theology of the incarnation—has an altogether peculiar meaning when we consider it from the point of view of the Church. If this fullness is understood as implying a certain infinity (cf. S.Th., 3ª,7,11), then only one conclusion is possible. This God-man must be the author or source of every *share* in God's life, the life of grace and truth.

Evidently, such a summary consideration of the origin of the mystery of the Church—namely in Jesus Christ—is wholly dependent on faith. Conviction concerning the Church is based on our belief that what St. John affirms—Christ is full of grace and truth—is true. From this we infer that somewhat the same relation exists between Christ and the life of grace shared by mankind as exists between God himself and the universe of being, which is but a participation in his infinite Being. We can say that Christ must be, as an "agent cause," the author of the Church.

CHRIST, IMAGE OF THE INVISIBLE GOD

St. Paul, the apostle of the gentiles, was deeply imbued with a sense of the primacy of Christ's authorship of the Church. We can benefit from meditating on some verses in the first chapter of his epistle to the Colossians, for it is there that he brings out another aspect of this primacy.

When Paul states that "all things have been created through and *unto him*" (Col. 1,16), he seems to be pointing out that, even as we share in the life of God in dependence upon Christ, so this same God-man is, as it were, the Omega to whom all God's gifts return. Nothing is exempt, neither "things visible [nor] things invisible, whether thrones, or dominations, or principalities, or powers." (*Ibid.*) This is to say that Jesus Christ is also the "final cause" of the Church, or that the Church has been created *for* him.

Certain attempts at precision are necessary at this point. Doubtless the Church exists for the glory of God. Here, however, we are interested in something not quite so remote or so absolutely final. This is the significance of calling the Church, the Church *of Christ*. Again the proportion between God and the universe of being on the one hand, and Christ and all the supernatural gifts of God on the other, helps us to understand what is involved. Just as God, the first cause of all things, in creating the universe intends to communicate some of his own perfection or goodness, so Christ, from the largesse of his sacred heart, pours forth the gifts of grace which somehow *make* the Church. Therefore, in the same way that we conclude that God's goodness is the final cause of all things (cf. *S.Th.*, 1ᵃ,44,4), we say the goodness of Christ is the Omega of the Church.

Here there is, as always, perfect correspondence between action and perfection. The Church is born from Christ's side, and she must return to him. He is the Alpha and the Omega.

CONFORMITY IN AND WITH CHRIST

Another favorite Pauline theme, which elucidates the total dependence of the Church upon Christ, is that of our *conformity* with him, that is, our being made over into his image. This theme is itself suggestive of yet a third facet of that dependence.

Here especially it is necessary to have recourse to an idea which is rooted in our faith concerning the blessed Trinity. It is this, namely that the Son of God, second person of the blessed Trinity, is generated of the Father as Wisdom. He is the Word: *Sapientia genita*. Furthermore, it is this Wisdom made flesh who is, as we have seen, the author of the "supernatural universe" which we call the Church.

In this light it is possible to see what is implied in the language of St. Paul when he says, for example, that we must become conformed to the image of God's Son (Rom 8,29); or, again, that "he will refashion the body of our lowliness, *conforming* it to the body of his glory." (Phil 3,21) The notion that underlies these expressions, or, at least, what we can derive from them, is that as Wisdom incarnate Jesus Christ is the grand pattern according to which the Church is formed. In other words,

9

the Church is "his idea"; all the elements that go to make it up reflect in some way, even though imperfectly, that Wisdom in which they have their source.

That the Church is an articulated image of the Word made flesh is verified first of all of the Church as a whole. In Christ the divine and human natures are united hypostatically in the person of the Word of God. He is true God and true man. In the Church this union of the divine and the human scarcely approaches the sublimity of *hypostatic* union, but the Church does image this union. She too is truly divine and truly human. In this way she is an image, though an imperfect one, of the incarnation itself. Precisely because Christ is a supreme and altogether transcendent exemplar, however, it is necessary that what he possesses simply and in perfect unity exist in the Church in multiple fashion and imperfectly. Thus the holiness of Christ is shared by each of his members—each in a different measure. This is what St. Paul means by the phrase, to be found "in Christ." (Cf. Phil 3,9) By the same token all of the functions of Christ, functions of the mission he received from the Father, are somehow mirrored in the Church.

Both these aspects, namely interior perfection and the visible articulation of the Church, are referred to by St. Paul in terms that make us certain that, in his mind, Christ *is* the first exemplar of the Church.

> And he himself gave some as apostles, and some as prophets, others again as evangelists, and others as pastors and teachers, in order to perfect the saints for a work of ministry for building up the body of Christ, until we all attain to the unity of faith and of the deep knowledge of the Son of God, to perfect manhood, to the mature measure of the fullness of Christ. (Eph 4,11ff)

Meditation on this key passage ties together what we have said about Christ as the goal, the author, and the pattern of the Church. First of all, it is *his* largesse which is the origin of whatever "perfects the saints." Then too, the largesse tends to the "mature measure of the fullness of Christ" as toward its final end. Lastly, he must be the apostle, the prophet, the evangelist, pastor, and teacher *par excellence.*

> For it has pleased the Father that in him all his fullness should dwell, and that through him he should reconcile to himself all things, whether on earth or in the heavens, making peace through the blood of the cross. (Col 1,19f)

CHAPTER TWO

CHRIST'S FOUNDATION OF THE CHURCH

THE NEW CREATION

One of the truths which has been the source of fruitful Christian contemplation in all ages is the unity of God's self-revelation. The traditional "history of salvation" goes back to the beginning of time. The Church has never thought otherwise. In a very concrete way she has always held that the same God is author of both the Old and New Testaments, that the "holy ones of both dispensations spoke under the inspiration of the same Holy Spirit." (D706)

This continuity of divine revelation—a continuity that in no way precludes gradual development—is made evident in a striking way if we compare the first verses of the Old Testament with the initial statements of St. John's gospel. The author of the book of Genesis begins his story in this way: *"In the beginning* God created the heavens and the earth." (Gn 1,1) Likewise St. John, the evangelist whose gospel might be called the most comprehensively theological, starts out: *"In the beginning* was the Word. . . ."* (Jn 1,1) He is obviously employing the same form or style, and this device suggests that the story he has to tell is like that which unfolds in the first pages of the Bible.

This supposition is a valid one, for the mission of Christ was to renew the face of the earth, to establish a new creation. The Word, through whom all things were made, having assumed flesh in the womb of the Virgin, was to remake the universe.

It is important, however, to complement this truth with another, namely, that the work of Christ—this new creation—is also quite distinctive. The darkness which covered the face of the earth when God said "Let there be light" can surely be compared to the darkness of which St. John speaks: "And the light shines in the darkness; and the darkness grasped it not." (Jn 1,5)

Perhaps the best way to bring out the distinctive character of Christ's *new* creation is by considering the Pauline terms with which we closed the previous chapter. St. Paul says that it was the will of God through Christ to *"reconcile* to himself all things . . . making peace through the blood of the cross." (Col 1,20) This gives us a clue to the real nature of the new creation.

The author of Genesis was constrained to represent the state of things before creation as dark and chaotic. "Nothing" has no meaning for us, and *nothing* was the starting point (*terminus a quo*) of the first creation.

St. Paul and St. John, however, were not laboring under the same difficulty in putting their finger on the state of things when God acted through Christ to remake the world. It was dark and chaotic in the strict sense because of the intervention and propagation of moral evil —sin—in the world God had created. This chaos consisted in the estrangement of man from God and the consequent enmity of men among themselves. Therefore, Christ's work was to be one of reconciliation, reparation, a putting into order, a creating of peace or a new paradise.

An excellent summation of the state of affairs which obtained when Christ came is that of St. Paul in the first part of his epistle to the Romans. (1,18–3,20) He shows conclusively that the entire world, pagan (1,18–32) as well as Jewish (2,1–3,20), was subject to the "wrath of God." The divine anger, moreover, manifests itself principally in the astounding growth of sinfulness, until he is forced to affirm, quoting the psalmist: "There is not one just man; there is not one that understands; there is not one that seeks after God. All have gone astray together; they have become worthless. There is not one who does good, no, not even one." (Rom 3,10ff)

The *terminus a quo*, therefore, of this new creation is, according to the apostle Paul, the absence of all justice, of all understanding, and the lack of any investigation of the ways of God. In a general way, evil seems to have prevailed, and "darkness truly covers the face of the earth."

"But when the *fullness of time* came, God sent his Son, born of a woman, born under the Law, that he might redeem those who were under the Law, that we might receive the adoption of sons." (Gal 4,4f) This is precisely the text that St. Thomas cites in order to establish that Christ came at the right time—not too early, in order that mankind might know what it means to be estranged from God and from his true self, and not too late, so that the fervor of love might still be ignited. (Cf. *S.Th.*, 3ª,1,5 and parallel texts.) The mission of Christ, therefore, was threefold—to fulfill all justice (Mt 3,15), to see to it that men might understand the "mind of the Lord" (1 Cor 2,16), to overcome, as the divine hero, the darkness which covered the face of the earth.

Reference to this Pauline text concerning the "fullness of time" indicates somewhat the limits of our study of the Church. It is in a certain sense true, as St. Augustine says, that the Church is present in the world "from the just Abel to the very end of time." (*Sermo* 341,9,11 [*PL* 39, 1499]) The Church of Christ was certainly prefigured in many ways in the Old Testament; the grace of God, working in virtue of the foreseen merits of Christ, was present to all men. Yet our interest will be centered upon the Church insofar as it has its beginning in the "fullness of time"—that moment in history when the Word took flesh in the womb of Mary. This is the new creation for which Christ himself is responsible.

Without digressing from our main theme, it seems appropriate *13* to say a word here about the "woman" whom St. Paul mentions in the text on the fullness of time. The passage indicates that in its very origin the mystery of the Church is bound up intimately with the mystery of our Lady; for she is the woman. That reconciliation which Christ came to accomplish, and which is in a certain sense the intrinsic perfection of the Church, was perfectly accomplished in Mary. Thus, as mother of the incarnate Word our Lady is the firstfruits of Christ's mission to reconcile all things to God. If the Church is the new creation and the new paradise, she is these things *par excellence*. This is a theme, in fact, which some of the Fathers of the Church have been at pains to develop. (Cf., St. John Damascene, *On the Dormition*, 9,1,8 [*PG* 96, 712].) In modern times this parallel between the mystery of the Church and the mystery of our Lady has been explored to such an extent that one author has said that,

> As far as the Christian mind is concerned, Mary is the "ideal figure of the Church", the "sacrament" of it and the "mirror in which the whole Church is reflected". Everywhere the Church finds in her its type and model, its *point of origin and perfection*. . . . (H. de Lubac, *The Splendour of the Church* [New York: Sheed and Ward, 1956], p. 242, italics added)

To sum up, we should say that the Wisdom of God is revealed first of all in that act wherein Christ, the author of the Church, begins to exist in his human nature. In the *fullness of time,* at a moment of history chosen by God as the most appropriate, the Son of God took flesh in the Virgin's womb, and thus constituted a new creation. All of the perfection of the Church, her beauty, the entire complex of action of which she is the subject, has its source in that moment.

HISTORICAL MOMENTS
OF THE NEW CREATION

The fact that St. Paul never laid eyes on our Lord during his earthly life is significant. This resulted in an extremely personal viewpoint on the life and work of Christ, through which Paul is easily distinguished from the evangelists.[1] He seems to have understood the new

14

---

[1] This statement is not to be taken as an affirmation that there is a "Pauline or Hellenistic Christianity" as distinguished from a Christianity which is "Johannine or

creation achieved through the God-man as one single act much in the same way as the author of Genesis portrayed the creative act of God. "In the beginning God created the heavens and the earth." (Gn 1,1) This insight is brought out well in a passage of the epistles to the Hebrews in which the author shows how it is Christ's simple acceptance of his mission which establishes what we have called the new creation.

> And then saying, "Behold I come to do your will, O God," he annuls the first covenant in order to establish the second. It is in this "will" that we have been sanctified through the offering of the body of Jesus Christ once for all. (Heb 10,9f)

Certainly it is true that this "once for all" was accomplished in germ at the very moment of the incarnation. It is there that Christ, by an act of his human will, ratified the will of the Father to reconcile all things to himself in his Son. Yet it is equally true that the revelation of this interior act and its articulation, as it were, took place over the span of years during which Christ dwelt among us, and especially in those climactic events to which Christ referred as his "hour." (Cf. Jn 2,4; 7,30; 8,20; 12,23.27; 13,1; 17,1.) [2] Our final consideration of Christ's causality in regard to the Church, therefore, will have to do with these years and these events.

Pope Pius XII, in his encyclical *Mystici Corporis*, was quite explicit in delineating the various moments which must here be taken into account.

> The Divine Redeemer began the building of the mystical temple of the Church when by His preaching he announced His precepts; He completed it when He hung glorified on the Cross; and he manifested and proclaimed it when he sent the Holy Ghost as Paraclete in visible form on his disciples. (*The Mystical Body of Christ*, encyclical letter of Pope Pius XII, introduction and notes by J. Bluett. [3d ed.; New York: America Press, 1957], par. 33, p. 20.)

Judaic." Such was the thesis of men like von Harnack and the modernists at the turn of the century. We mean, rather, that St. Paul's personal assimilation of the one gospel was in accord with his own temperament and environment and experience, and that it complements, in God's providence, the viewpoint of those who were eye-witnesses of Christ's Pasch. Actually, St. Paul did see the glorious Christ on the road to Damascus. (Cf. Ac 9,1ff.)

[2] A period between verse numbers indicates that the verses cited are successive but nonconsecutive.

We shall proceed from Christ's public ministry to his crucifixion to his fruitful glorification as it is seen on Pentecost.

The Public Life of Christ

It is doubtless impossible to reconstruct perfectly the chronological sequence of events of the two or three years of Christ's life, simply because the evangelists were not writing a biography in the modern sense. It is sufficient for us, in studying the Church, to discern in the gospels themselves incidents in Christ's life and words of his which, if interpreted in the light of Christian tradition, give some indication of his will for the Church.

Among these incidents, the first concerns Christ's choice of a group of men who were to be called "apostles," that is, those who are sent, and who, in the primitive Christian community, were known as "the Twelve." St. Luke clearly indicates that this act of Christ was of primary importance:

> . . . in those days . . . he went out to the mountain to pray, and continued all night in prayer to God. And when day broke, he summoned his disciples; and from these he chose twelve (whom he also named apostles): Simon, whom he named Peter, and his brother Andrew; James and John; Philip and Bartholomew; Matthew and Thomas; James, the son of Alpheus, and Simon called the Zealot; Jude the brother of James, and Judas Iscariot, who turned traitor. (Lk 6,12–16; cf. Mk 3,14–19; Mt 10,1–4.)

We cannot help being struck by the solemnity with which Christ performs this action—his night-long vigil, the discerning of *twelve* from among all those who followed him, and the special name with which they were designated. Nor can we refrain from seeing here a figure of what might be called the tragic element in the mystery of the Church: "Judas Iscariot, who turned traitor," the first unworthy minister in the new creation.

St. Matthew adds a note which suggests another idea: ". . . having summoned his twelve disciples, he gave them *power* over unclean spirits, to cast them out, and to cure every kind of disease and infirmity," (Mt 10,1), a note which he completes at the very end of his gospel when there were only eleven.

Go, therefore, and make disciples of all nations, baptizing them in the name of the Father, and of the Son, and of the Holy Spirit, teaching them to observe all that I have commanded you; and behold, I am with you all days, even unto the consummation of the world. (Mt 28,18ff; cf. Mk 16,15f; Ac 1,8.)

Pope Pius XII says authoritatively that these words and events are evidence that Christ sent his apostles, "as He had been sent by the Father, namely as teachers, rulers, instruments of holiness in the assembly of the believers." (*Op. cit.*, par. 34)

There is one detail in the accounts of the election of the apostles, the significance of which mounts as we consider the ensemble of witnesses concerning the foundation of the Church both in the gospels and in the story of the growth of the nascent Church in the Acts of the Apostles. At the head of the list of the Twelve (and this is true of every list) is that "Simon, whom he named Peter." It is quite certain that previous to that time the name Peter (*Kepha,* "the Rock"), was not used as the name of a man. In any case, we have other evidence which clarifies what was in Christ's mind, whenever he chose to make this change.

The texts on which the Catholic Church bases her belief in the primacy of Peter as the Vicar of Christ on earth are well known: Mt 16,18f; Lk 22,31f; Jn 21,15–17. Whatever the precise meaning of this primacy may be—a thing to be determined in the light of tradition and under the guidance of the Church's teaching—this designation of Simon is something that Christ did to found his Church.

The gospels in their entirety are a witness that our Lord, while fulfilling his office as preacher, transmitted to his apostles a deposit of faith which they in turn were to keep intact and to pass on to succeeding generations.

Finally, there are clear indications in the gospels that Christ established or instituted certain sacred rites which were to be the sacraments *of the Church.* Principal among these were baptism, "by which those who should believe would be incorporated in the Body of the Church," (Pius XII, *ibid.*), and the wonderful sacrifice and sacrament of the eucharist.

The choice of the apostles and the designation of Peter as the head of the apostolic company, the teaching of the truths which were to be the object of Christian faith, and the institution of sacraments which were to be the source of Christian life are the significant acts of Christ through which he began the foundation or creation of his Church.

On the Cross

In order to understand how the creation of the Church, begun in the years of Christ's preaching activity, was perfected on the gibbet of the cross, we must recall that the circumstances of the "fullness of time" were quite peculiar. Up to this point we have spoken of Christ as Wisdom incarnate, Son of God and Son of the Virgin. To restrict our view, however, to these truths would be to neglect another important truth: our God is the God of history, and he providentially arranged all the events which went before Christ's coming in such a way that they were ordered to this one Christ-event.

This is especially true of the history of God's chosen people, the Jews, with whom Yahweh had made a covenant. (Cf. Gn 15;17;19;21, 1–21.) The mission of the incarnate Word of God involved fulfillment of this covenant and the Law which was its adjunct. (Cf. Mt 5,17ff.) In other words, our Lord was a son of Abraham. The very name which was claimed for him, the *Christ,* was the fulfillment of all the hopes of Israel. He was the Messia, the Anointed One of whom the prophets had spoken. He was to establish a new and everlasting covenant for his people and for all nations. (Cf. Mt 26,63ff; also Jer 31,31–34.)

Now, the fact that the Church was, as it were, "born from the side of Our Savior on the Cross . . ." (Pius XII, *ibid.*) is so well established in Christian tradition that we may take it as a sort of principle. The reasons for this affirmation are either directly or indirectly connected with the mystery of Christ's Jewish origins.

The first of these reasons is dramatically pointed out by the evangelist, who tells how, at the moment of Christ's death the veil of the Temple was mysteriously ripped from top to bottom. (Mt 27,51; cf. Heb 9,12; 10,20) This incident is traditionally understood as the definitive inauguration of the worship of the new covenant, the "messianic sanctuary" which is the Body of Christ himself. In other words, the death of Christ on Calvary was the final ratifying of the groundwork that he had laid during his public life, especially where sacramental worship is concerned.

18

By the same token, through his death Christ took complete possession of the entire human race, opening up to all nations the immense treasury of grace which is to be found in him. And finally, as Pius XII teaches, "through his blood . . . the Church was endowed with that fullest communication of the Holy Spirit through which . . . she is divinely illumined." (*Op. cit.*, par. 38, p. 21) These are the reasons for which we say that what Christ began in the countryside of Galilee and Judea with respect to the Church, he completed on the hill of Calvary.

On Pentecost

In the cycle of the Church's year, the significance of the Pentecostal feast has been most misunderstood. Many Christians tend to think of it simply as the "feast of the Holy Ghost." As a matter of fact, there is no such special commemoration of the Holy Ghost apart from the Father and the Son, any more than there is a feast of either of these other two persons of the august Trinity taken singly.

The real meaning of Pentecost is connected rather with the mystery we are at present contemplating: the perfect accomplishment of Christ's will to establish the new creation. It is true that the presence of the Holy Spirit in the Church had been promised by Christ in the last discourse of his public life. (Cf. Jn 16,4b–15) We have also affirmed that this promise was fulfilled by the shedding of Christ's blood on the cross. Now, however, we can conclude that Wisdom incarnate, having come into the possession of his kingdom, willed to make manifest to the entire world the power and the beauty of the new creation of which he is the author. This he did in the mystery of the visible mission of the Holy Spirit, the soul of the Church. (Cf. Ac 2,1–13)

If one reads the entire chapter in which this work of God is told, it is impossible not to be struck by how all that we have said about the founding work of Christ is synthesized. It is *Peter* who stands up (v.14) and delivers the first apostolic invitation to the world: "Men of Judea and all you who dwell in Jerusalem, let this be known to you and give ear to my words." (*Ibid.*) In this sermon the prince of the apostles courageously points out the meaning of Christ's mission. The heart of it all is his reference to the crucified and risen Jesus. (vv.22ff) Later in this same chapter (vv42–46), there is a description of the life of the Church in Jerusalem in which all these elements are again in evidence

—the teaching of the apostles and the breaking of the bread, undoubtedly a reference to the eucharistic celebrations of these first Christians. "And each day the Lord added to the community those who were to be saved." (47b) The creative work of Christ is complete. The Church has been constituted a *living organism*.

CHAPTER THREE

BIBLICAL IMAGES

If our first two chapters may be described as "beginnings" with respect to the Wisdom of God and the constitution of the Church, the next three (3, 4, 5) are fittingly described as concerned with "order and distinction" in the Church. To say that the deposit of faith is transmitted to us in the Church through symbols is to affirm that God has accommodated himself, has stooped to our lowliness, in order to make his truth intelligible. Even the baptismal formulas convey the inexpressible truths of Christian faith by way of verbal analogy. That which is wholly spiritual, and therefore wholly intelligible in itself, is given to us clothed in figures. The function of the Church in guarding the development of faith is to determine the sense of these symbols or figures. One of the functions of theology in the Church is to penetrate more deeply into their meaning.[1]

The richness of the mystery of the Church is such that one symbol or figure could not adequately express its depths. For that matter, neither do all the figures taken together adequately delineate the visage of the Church. We can be sure, however, that God has provided the figures which are most appropriate for the discovery of these riches. Our task in this chapter is, first, to collect the data of revelation wherein the mystery of the Church is *symbolically* portrayed; then, by reflection, to see what characteristics of the Church, common or peculiar, are suggested by the symbols in question.

FIVE FIGURES OF THE CHURCH

The Church as Kingdom

This first of the biblical images of the Church is one that pervades all of God's revelation. Its application to the Church has its roots in the Old Testament. God's royal sovereignty over the entire universe, which is expressed in many of the psalms (cf. Ps 92[93], 96[97], 98[99]), came to have particular significance for the chosen people. According to the theocratic ideal of the Old Testament, Yahweh was their King. In the postexilic book of Daniel there is foretold the establishment of a "kingdom that shall never be destroyed, and [this] kingdom shall not be delivered up to another people, and it shall break in pieces and shall consume all these kingdoms, and itself shall stand forever." (Dn 2,44) The fulfillment of this prophecy began approximately two hundred years later with the coming of the messianic King, Jesus Christ.

No doubt the best possible way of steeping ourselves in the knowl-

---

[1] St. Thomas explains the reason for the use of metaphors, figures or symbols of God in revelation in the S.Th., 1ª,1,9; cf. also 3 *Contra Gentes*, where he shows how our return to God is also via symbols, in this case the sacraments, the worship life of the Church.

edge of this image of the Church, the preliminary to understanding its meaning, is to read and meditate upon the gospel of St. Matthew. This is the theme that seems to be uppermost in his mind. P. Benoit has called this entire gospel "a drama on the coming of the kingdom of heaven in seven acts."[2] The coming of the kingdom is announced by John the Baptist (Mt 3,2), and then by Christ himself. (Mt 4,17) This gospel ends, too, on a regal note: "All power on heaven and earth has been given to me." (Mt 28,18) Later we shall reflect on the meaning of this symbol in connection with the order that Christ the King gave to his new creation, the Church.

The Church as Temple of God

The texts of the Bible in which this second figure is set forth are the following: 1 Cor 3,10–17; 2 Cor 6,16ff; Eph 2,14–22 (Cf. Y. M.-J. Congar, *Le Mystère du Temple*, "Lectio Divina," 22; Eng. tr., *The Mystery of the Temple*. Baltimore: Helicon, 1962). Again, the roots of this image are planted in the Old Testament. St. Paul was well aware that the temple in Jerusalem was both the center of Israel's worship and the symbol of that nation's hope for the fulfillment of the prophet's promises:

> Therefore, thus says
> the Lord God:
> See, I am laying a stone
> in Sion,
> A precious cornerstone as a
> sure foundation.
> (Is 28,16)

Still, there is something quite unique in this Pauline adaptation of the image, namely, that the community of believers in Christ constitutes the temple, the house of God, the place in which God dwells. Once again we can sense the importance of drawing from this image some understanding of the order and constitution of the new creation established by Christ.

23

---

[2] Introduction to the gospel of St. Matthew, *La Sainte Bible,* traduite en français sous la direction de l'École Biblique de Jérusalem (Paris: Éditions du Cerf, 1956), p. 1287.

The Church as Spouse of Christ

The images by which the Church has been portrayed up to this point might very well be called "material." This is to say that, even though St. Peter speaks of the faithful as "living stones" of a "spiritual house" (1 Pt 2,5), nevertheless the idea of an organic or "biological" constitution is absent from the figures of kingdom and temple, as such. To conceive of them as living, having an inner dynamism, is to go beyond the limits of the image, and this we can do only by virtue of other biblical symbols of the Church.

Married people in the Church ought to be especially fond of the image which St. Paul calls "a great mystery" (Eph 5,32)—the comparison he draws between the union of husband and wife in Christian marriage and that which obtains between Christ and his Church. (vv. 25–32) This is surely a living symbol, in which two human persons who have become one flesh stand in the place of incarnate Wisdom and his mystical spouse. To understand how the Church is Christ's spouse is to penetrate deeply the reality of the Church's organic structure.

The Church as Vine

The symbol of the Church which is strictly Johannine is one that we have from the lips of Christ himself. (Jn 15,1–9.16) Perhaps it portrays more clearly than the previous image the total dependence of the Church upon Christ: "Without me you can do nothing." (v.5) Similarly, however, Christ's affirmation that he is the true vine of which we are the branches is an excellent example of the deficiency of any and all symbols designed to show truth concerning the mystery. We might say that, from one point of view, the union of vine and branch is *too close* to convey the meaning of Christ's union with the Church; after all, in the vine the branch has no individuality of its own. From another point of view, however, the image is *too weak;* for the mystical union of Christ with the members of his Church, consisting as it does in a supernatural bond, is infinitely more sublime than the merely physical union of vine and branch. Here theology's guide is, as always, the Church's own understanding and determination of the *sense* of the image.

24

The Church as Christ's Body

There is no image or figure of the Church "more sublime or more Divine" than that which portrays her as Christ's own body—his mystical body.[3] (Cf. Pius XII, *op. cit.*, par. 17, p. 16.) The author of this symbol seems to be St. Paul; and in order to become familiar with it, one must read at least the following passages from his epistles: Rom 12,4f; 1 Cor 12,12–31; Eph 1,22; 5,23.30; Col. 1,18.24.

Here is an image that has no counterpart in the Old Testament, an image however which is the object of the Church's most intense reflection. This meditation culminated, as it were, in the encyclical letter of Pope Pius XII, *Mystici Corporis,* which will be for us the source of innumerable lights concerning the organic structure and the life of the Church.

MEANING OF THE FIVE FIGURES

The interpretations of all these symbols, which can be made only according to the so-called "analogy of faith," that is, under the guidance of the Church's grasp of the entire ensemble of divinely revealed truths, follows certain general principles. In the first place, there is something metaphorical about them. In metaphorical expressions, the subject of the metaphor cannot be made to conform in every way to the reality with which it is identified. Thus, for example, when it is said that Christ is the head of his body, that is, has absolute primacy over it, it remains true that Christ himself, in his human nature, is subject to God who has the primacy in all things. (Cf. *S.Th.*, 3ᵃ,8,1, ad 2.)

The value of the symbols, therefore, lies in the possibility of our seeing in them certain likenesses which enable us to penetrate to the reality of the mystery of the Church. With the revealed symbols at hand we shall discuss these likenesses under the following headings: the presence of a *principle of order* or distinction in the Church; the *multiplicity of elements* that go to make up the single reality, which is the

---

[3] For a discussion of the history of the use of the term "mystical" in reference to the Church, see also H. de Lubac, "The Heart of the Church," *op. cit.*, pp. 87-113.

Church; the *variety of functions* which is implied in the symbols; the *dynamism* inherent in the Church, which may be inferred from these same symbols. Finally we shall draw some general conclusions with regard to the *order* established in the new creation by its author, Wisdom incarnate.

A Principle of Order in the Church

Christ is the immediate principle of all order and distinction in the Church. It does not matter which of the many images we take first; they each bring us immediately to the truth that Christ is both author of the Church and the one who gives her the perfection of order—the greatest of all perfections. This is certainly the function of a king in relation to his domain. Those who govern are required to put things in their proper place, and to do so with authority. Such authority is verified most of all in the case of Christ the King, up to that moment at the end of time "when he delivers the kingdom to God the Father, when he does away with all sovereignty, authority, and power. For he must reign until 'he has put all his enemies under his feet.'" (1 Cor 15,24f) With all due proportion the same may be said of the husband in the family, whose practical wisdom, a share in the wisdom of the Father, is the principle of order in the household.

When St. Paul adapts the temple image to designate the Church he makes Christ's key position explicit in a somewhat different context. He calls our Lord the "chief cornerstone" (Eph 2,20), apparently being possessed of the idea that the "two peoples," Jew and gentile, who up to that moment had been separated by an "intervening wall" (v. 14), are now part of the same building—and this because of their being joined to Christ. "In him the whole structure is closely fitted together. . . ." (v. 21)

One common trait of Christ's principality that is evident in all of these images is the paradoxical truth that at the same time Christ is *over and above* the Church and also *in* the Church. King, husband, and chief cornerstone: all these symbols indicate a certain pre-eminence; but at the same time they do not exclude intimate cohesion between the principle and that which comes under its influence. Of course, Christ has two claims to this pre-eminence: first, he is the eternal Son of God; second, his sacred humanity is full of grace. "Grace is conferred upon

26

the soul of Christ as upon a certain *universal* principle." (*S.Th.*, 3ª,7,11) His inclusion within the Church, moreover, is based upon his being true man, that is, really one of us.

This paradox is particularly relevant to the symbol which represents Christ as the head of his *body* which is the Church. In the physical body the head has, without doubt, the first place. St. Thomas analyzes this pre-eminence and distinguishes three ways in which it is verified: (1) as to *order,* the head is at the "top"; (2) where *perfection* is concerned, the head is the place in which all the senses and motive powers are present, whereas in other parts of the body they are diffused; (3) finally, because of this perfection the head is in some manner directive, having influence over the rest of the members. (*S.Th.*, 3ª,8,1) Now if, as St. Thomas affirms, these three properties of headship are verified spiritually in Christ (*ibid.*), it is not the less true that, even as the head of a physical body remains a member of the body, although the first member, so Christ is the chief member of the Church.

The truth that we are trying to establish here is that the reality which we call the Church is radically associated with a single principle of order. This principle may be symbolized in various ways, but if we examine the mystery there is only one to whom these symbolic principles —king, cornerstone, husband, vine, head—can possibly correspond: Jesus Christ.

Multiplicity of Elements Making Up the Church

Of all the symbols by which the Church is represented, that of bride of Christ seems the least apt to represent multiplicity. Perhaps this is the reason that in the Apocalypse, where the author is speaking of the consummation of all things, he returns to this image. (Cf. Ap 21,2; 22,17.) In this last and everlasting moment the Church will have attained her ultimate unity, "perfect manhood, . . . the mature measure of the fullness of Christ." (Eph 4,13) The Church is conceived of as distinct from Christ but as a single person united to him in one flesh. (Cf. Eph 5,30.)

The other images, however, make it quite clear that there must be multiplicity in the Church. A body has *many* members; a temple is built from *many* stones (cf. 1 Pt 2,5); a healthy vine bears *many* 27 branches, some of which are fruitful and others not. Even in the parables of Christ, in which he devised other symbols concerning the Kingdom of heaven, there are indications of the necessity of this multiplicity. There are seeds of various kinds (cf. Mt 13,3b-9), wheat and weeds (vv.24–30), and many species of fish (vv. 47–50), all in the one kingdom.

Variety of Functions in the Church

These same images indicate that the multiplicity in the one Church is not merely a *numerical distinction,* whether of members, living stones, or fruitful branches. Inequality, or *specific distinction* of organic function, is also involved and, we might say, absolutely necessary. In some of the symbols this idea is expressed clearly; in others it seems to be implied.

St. Paul spells out the division of labor in the Church by extending the metaphor of the Church as the body of Christ. "Not all the members have the same function" (Rom 12,4); and again, "God has so tempered the body together in due proportion . . . that the members may have care one for another." (1 Cor 12,24f; cf. Col 2,19; Eph 4,11ff.)

The same may be said of the temple image. The Apostle tells the Corinthians that his function in the Church was, "as a wise builder," to lay the foundations. (1 Cor 3,10) Others are called to build upon it. And we may infer from the later adaptation of this same image (1 Pt 2,5), that the function of some in the Church is simply *to be* living stones, that is, to be part of the building without, perhaps, doing anything remarkable. It is important to be quite convinced that this is a function, in the Church and of the Church, for Peter is quick to add here that the total effect of this cohesion of living stones is "a spiritual house, a holy priesthood, to offer spiritual sacrifices acceptable to God through Jesus Christ." (*Ibid.*)

Other applications of this notion to the Church seem to be more adventitious. For example, Christ once told a parable about the "laborers in the vineyard" (Mt 20,1ff), which complements, but only implicitly, the image of the vine. By the same token, St. Paul speaks of espousals within the Church as a union of Christ with a "chaste virgin." (2 Cor 11,2; cf. 1 Cor 7,25ff) This might suggest to us that even in the Church the state of virginity is an ecclesial function; but it would

28

seem to be wrong to derive this notion directly from the image which is fundamental, namely that of husband and bride.

In any case it is quite certain, on the basis of symbols that are revealed, that there is specific diversity in the living organism which is the Church, and that this inequality is necessary for the common good of this organism. From this diversity of function the Church "derives its increase to the building up of itself in love."

The Dynamism Inherent in the Church

Two truths lead us to the last application of the biblical images to the mystery of the Church. The first is a principle of order or distinction that is visible in the Church, and the second is that this distinction consists both in a numerical multitude and an organically cohesive variety of functions. The body is growing. All its members, but most of all the head, contribute to this growth. (Cf. Eph 4,16.) Christ sanctifies his bride with a view to her being "holy and without blemish." (Eph 5,27b) The temple is not completed; the foundations are laid, but it is still in the process of construction. The kingdom of Christ is engaged in a titanic struggle with another kingdom, that of Satan. (Cf. Mt 12,25f.) Finally, Christ the vine is glorified in that those whom he has chosen "bear very much fruit." (Jn 15,8.16)

Wisdom, incarnate Wisdom, "has built her house, she has set up her seven columns." (Prv 9,1) To this extent the Church is already perfect. Yet, through her intimate union with Christ the principle of order and because of the capacity for perfection on the part of her members—and still more because there is an entire humanity to be perfected, dispersed throughout space and time—the Church is in a state of dynamism. She is growing up "in all things in him who is the head, Christ." (Eph 4,15)

THE SIGNIFICANCE OF BIBLICAL IMAGERY

What are the conclusions which may be drawn from this consideration of the real meaning of the biblical symbols concerning the Church? In the first place, we should say, once again, that Christ the divine Wisdom is the cause of the distinction and order to be found in

29

the new creation. To be sure, since the Church is a reality which has its source in a free act of God, it would have been impossible for us to predict prior to her institution the precise nature of that order. The knowledge of that is entirely dependent upon God's revelation. Yet, we can say that since the principle of this order, Jesus Christ, is possessed of the infinite treasures of divine goodness, and is at the same time the Wisdom eternally begotten, his body, and bride, and kingdom, will have to share in a multiple and divided manner that which he has simply and uniformly. In this respect there is again perfect correspondence between the universe of created reality in relation to God and the new creation in relation to Christ:

> The distinction of things and their multiplicity is intended by God, the first *Agens*. This is because he caused things to be in order both to communicate his goodness to creatures and also, through them, to make it manifest. Now God's goodness cannot sufficiently be represented by a single creature; and so he created many having diverse natures, that what is lacking to one in the manifestation of divine goodness might be supplied by another; for the goodness of which God is possessed simply and uniformly is present in creatures in multiple and diverse fashion. (*S.Th.*, 1ª,47,1)

We can gain a great insight into the nature of the Church, the mystical body of Christ, if we substitute in this text Christ for God, and the Church (new creation) for the ensemble of created things, all due proportion being observed.

Nor does it seem out of place to re-emphasize that it is not merely a matter of numerical distinctions. Diversity of function and inequality in dignity are also demanded by the nature of the Church, as being born from the heart of Christ, "full of *goodness* and love, in which are all the treasures of *wisdom* and knowledge." The head is not the eye, nor is the eye the ear or the foot. Each one has its proper function; all are necessary. In other words the Church is not an egalitarian society, an association of men who band together because of something they have in common, with the understanding that no one is to have authority over anyone else. It is at no time assumed that everyone will be on an equal footing. Furthermore, St. Paul calls our attention to the paradox that "those that seem the more feeble members of the body are more necessary." (1 Cor 12,22)

30

This same paradox introduces us to the last conclusion, which is at once an object of faith and of theological understanding. Every Sunday we sing or recite at Mass the creed in which we reaffirm our unshakeable belief in the *one, holy, catholic* Church. Here we are interested in penetrating that conviction, in seeing some of the reasons for which the affirmation is made, without pretending to make it any less an object of faith.

Certainly the catholicity of the Church can be understood better in terms of the distinction and inequality—*ordered* distinction and *ordered* inequality—which we have seen to be necessary to her perfection. This is to say that the Church's catholicity is not, in the first place, a matter of geographical extension. It is rather to be understood, first, in connection with the intention of the author of the Church, Jesus Christ, that she be a multiple and diverse manifestation of the infinite goodness and wisdom. This is what St. Paul means when he says that the Church is the "completion (*plē′rōma*) of him who fills all in all." (Eph 1,23) The Church's is the "fullness" of Christ. Thus she is capable, through her spouse's love with which he has endowed her, of drawing all things to herself. This makes her "catholic," that is, sharing in the fullness of Christ.

The Church's unity is the other side of the coin. Perhaps it would be well to cite again St. Thomas's expression of it: "The unity of the Church has two aspects, (1) the connection of the members one with the other, or *communication*, (2) and, again the *ordering* of all the members of the Church to one head." (S.Th., 2ª,2ᵃᵉ,39,1) We may call the unity which St. Thomas means by *communicatio* the Church's organic unity; that which he designates "order," we may call her moral unity. It is evident that this distinction is derived immediately from St. Thomas's contemplation of the biblical image, the body of Christ.

The Church's organic unity is such that all the members of the Church live one life; "one body and one spirit, even as you were called in one hope of your calling." (Eph 4,4) In this respect the unity of the Church is something that is interior and invisible; its principle is the life of grace and her invisible soul the Holy Spirit. This is not to say that it does not manifest itself externally. The immediate effect of this organic bond of members of Christ one with the other is that they "practice the truth in love." (Eph 4,15a)

The moral unity of the Church, however, or "unity of order" is

31

by definition a *visible* unity. The members of the Church are human persons and their cohesion in one society, with an order to a single head, must be visible. (Cf. Leo XIII, encyclical letter, *Satis cognitum*, on the unity of the Church [*ASS*, 28 (1895–96), 708–39], par. 3.) We shall see that many of the elements in the Church's life are visible, and that this is in perfect accord with the nature of her members.

These two aspects of the unity of the Church are not opposed. Rather, they answer perfectly to the demands made by the images with which we began, some of which indicated an external structure while others were "biological" and suggested that the unity of the Church is something more divine and sublime than we can possibly imagine or think.[4]

---

[4] In connection with the study of the Church's unity it is necessary to read the section of Pius XII's encyclical, *Mystici corporis* which deals with this aspect of the mystery. Cf. *op. cit.*, pars. 73-99, pp. 35-41.

CHAPTER FOUR

MEMBERSHIP
IN THE CHURCH

The title of this chapter shows how deeply embedded the theology of the Church is in biblical imagery. It is not a question of our having used these symbols once for all, in order to abstract precise notions about the Church. We must have recourse to them constantly, always with a view to penetrating their "catholic" sense.

The image which seems most aptly to suggest the direction of the present chapter is, strangely enough, not that of the body of Christ, even though the word "membership" is derived from it. The parallel to membership in the kingdom image is made evident by St. Paul as follows: "[God] has rescued us from the powers of darkness and *transferred* us into the kingdom of his beloved Son, in whom we have redemption, the remission of sins." (Col 1,13f) [Italics added] This is the idea which we wish to exploit. The apostle here speaks of our entry into the kingdom (cf. Mt 5,20) in terms of a *transfer*—looking at it from the point of view of God's action, or a *passage*, viewing it as the effect of the divine action in us—from one kingdom to another. The presupposition is that all mankind is, in the present circumstances, subject to a tyrannical lord (cf. Eph 2,1–3), and that Christ, author of the new creation, has broken these bonds and led us into the kingdom of the new covenant. (Cf. Mt 12,25–30.) In other words, entry into the kingdom, which is equivalent to membership in the Church, is a term which designates that perfection by which those who are created anew by the grace of Christ are distinguished from the "children of wrath." Our task in this chapter, therefore, is to delineate the conditions of this "distinction of perfection." Furthermore, because of the difficulties which have arisen throughout the history of the Church on this point, we shall also have to discuss the famous axiom, *extra ecclesiam nulla salus.* ("There is no salvation outside the Church.") This will suggest certain points in connection with the position of our separated brothers and the significance of the ecumenical movement. Finally, since membership in Christ's body or entry into his kingdom designates the fundamental *perfection* of the new creation, we shall add a sort of appendix concerning one of the "states of perfection" in the Church, namely, the religious life.

CONDITIONS OF MEMBERSHIP
IN THE CHURCH

An altogether adequate starting point for our discussion is the description of membership which Pius XII gives in the encyclical, *Mystici Corporis:*

34

Only those are . . . members of the Church who (1) have been baptized and (2) profess the true faith and (3) who have not unhappily withdrawn from the body-unity or for grave faults been excluded by legitimate authority. . . . It follows that those who are divided in faith and government cannot be living in one Body such as this, and cannot be living the life of its one divine Spirit. (*Op. cit.*, par. 29, pp. 18f)

The whole question of membership in the Church really hinges on the understanding of the terms of this text.

The first positive point concerns the sacrament of baptism as prerequisite to entry into the kingdom which is the Church, the body of Christ. We might call this sacrament the "door to the Church," as it is also the "door" to the other sacraments. (*Janua sacramentorum*; cf. *S.Th.*, 3ª,69,7.)

There is, moreover, a truth underlying this affirmation which we ought not to miss, namely that membership in the Church is accomplished, first of all, by sacramental contact with him who is the *magnum sacramentum*, Jesus Christ.

We should be remiss in not pointing out that, from the very beginning, the Church is formed as a *sacramental reality*. There are three manifestations of this doctrine. First, Christ himself, in the mystery of the incarnation, is the sacrament *par excellence*. His visible human nature is the vessel and source of all invisible divine gifts. Second, the sacraments which he instituted—one of the most important elements in the history of the new creation—mirror this mystery of the invisible divine gifts, contained in and transmitted through visible signs. Finally, the Church whose membership is constituted through the sacraments, especially baptism and the eucharist, is a consummate image of this same mystery. She too is a sacrament, at once visible and invisible, divine and human.

The second condition included in Pius XII's definition of membership in the Church is *profession of the true faith*. It would be wrong to suppose that this condition is quite distinct from the first. Rather, it flows from it, for the sacrament of baptism is the *sacramentum fidei* or sacrament of faith. St. Paul mentions the two in one breath: "one Lord, *one faith, one baptism,* one God and Father of all, who is above all, and throughout all, and in us all." (Eph 4,6) And in the rite of baptism, the first question and answer in the dialogue between the minister of the Church and the catechumen are: "What do you seek from the Church of God? *Faith!*" Then, in the procession from the entrance of

35

the Church (symbolic of the portals leading to eternal life) to the baptismal font, the minister leads all present in the recitation of the Apostolic Creed. This is even before the waters of baptism perfect the catechumen's faith by setting upon it the seal of the baptismal character and making him a living stone in the temple of the Church. Baptism renders the catechumen capable of offering that spiritual sacrifice acceptable to God through Jesus Christ (cf. 1 Pt 2,5) which is a "profession of faith made unto salvation." (Rom 10,10) In other words the normal result of being incorporated into Christ by the sacramental rite is a witness to the great mystery of which baptism is the living and life-giving symbol.

Nor ought we to suppose that the negative restrictions which the pope adds to his description are merely juridical conditions. They are intimately connected with the foregoing, simply because baptism and the profession of the true faith imply the living of a *full* Christian life. In other words, when a person has been made a member of Christ and the Church through baptism, the normal response on his part is a public witness to his gratitude for God's gifts. This is a witness of faith and a witness of love, because membership in the Church is incorporation into a brotherhood or fellowship, the distinctive characteristic of which is fraternal love. (Cf. Jn 13,34f; 1 Jn 4,20f.)

There are, moreover, several ways in which one can lose membership in this mystical body of which Pius XII speaks. First of all, this can come about through the sin of heresy. (Cf. *S.Th.*, 2ª 2ᵃᵉ,11, for a discussion of the specific character of this sin.) The word "heresy" describes the situation wherein a person who has been baptized and has professed the true faith *chooses* to deny one or another of the articles of the faith that is taught by the Catholic Church. By that act he cuts himself off from membership in the Church, the body of Christ.

No one can fail to see how incompatible are membership in Christ's Church and the refusal to give assent to the teaching authority which he himself has founded. It is extremely important, however, to grasp a distinction which was expressed succinctly by St. Augustine, and which has become the common patrimony of Catholic theology. Here is what the Doctor of Grace says:

36   A person who defends his own opinion [in matters of faith], even though it be erroneous and perverse, but who defends it without obstinacy, especially when the [opinion] is not the fruit of his own per-

verse presumption, but is rather inherited from parents who have fallen into error; who, furthermore, is searching diligently for the truth, ready to surrender to it when he comes to know it—such a person is *not to be counted among the heretics.*" (*Epist.* 43, n.1 [*PL* 33,160])

The thought expressed here is clearly the basis for the distinction between "formal" and "material" heresy, or, if we are to adopt a more modern terminology, between heresy and "dissidence." Besides this, although speculation here is rather useless, we can presume that there are great numbers of "dissident Christians"—again, their separation is material rather than formal—who answer to St. Augustine's description. It is on the basis of this distinction that we must, at least in theory, conceive such Christians in relation to the body of Christ. It is "formal heresy," that is, willful defection from one or another article of faith, with a perverse preference for one's own opinion in contrast to the teaching of the Church, which separates a person from the body of the Church. *A fortiori,* of course, must this be said of the sin of apostasy, whereby a person rejects the entire body of Catholic truth in which he has been nurtured. (Cf. *S.Th.,* 2ª 2ᵃᵉ,12)

The second possible type of rupture from membership in the Church is the sin of schism. With due proportion, the same distinctions must be made here with respect to formal and material schism as have been made concerning heresy. (Cf. *S.Th.,* 2ª 2ᵃᵉ,39.) St. Thomas places this sin among those contrary to charity, the bond of perfection. Pius XII refers to this sin when he speaks of those who are divided from the Catholic Church in government, for just as a heretic opposes the Church's teaching, so the schismatic opposes her maternal function of guiding the faithful toward their common end. This too results in an *ipso facto* break with the body of Christ.[1]

Finally, it is possible for the Church herself, in the person of those who are possessed of legitimate authority, to take action against a mem-

---

[1] Although those whom we have called "dissidents," either on account of material heresy or material schism are surely "unsuspectingly . . . related in desire and resolution to the Mystical Body of the Redeemer" (*Mystici Corporis,* par. 121; *op. cit.,* p. 48), it seems clear that Pius XII wished that these Christians not be called *members* of the Church. Even though the search for a proper terminology to be applied here presents great difficulties, the reality of their relation to the Church, the mystical body, is undeniable.

ber guilty of grave fault. Such an exercise of her right—which has its roots in the authority and mission of the twelve apostles—is called an "excommunication." Although the juridical aspects of such ecclesiastical action have continued to develop through the centuries and modifications have taken place, there is, in the fifth chapter of St. Paul's first epistle to the Corinthians, an excellent example of excommunication.

These are the conditions, positive and negative, of membership in the Church, by which the "children of light" are distinguished from the "children of darkness." There is one remaining problem that ought to be discussed here even though we cannot hope to fathom the mystery of it. This is the ironical truth that there are sinners in the Church despite the fact that she is "holy and without blemish," the bride of Christ. (Eph 5,27b)

The teaching of the Church on this point could not be clearer. It is founded especially in the parables of Christ, in which our Lord speaks of the "wheat and the weeds" growing together to the end of the world (Mt 13,24–30; 36–43), or of the net cast into the sea "that gathered in fish of every kind." (Ibid., 47–50) Pius XII's words are an echo of these parables. "Not every sin . . . is such as to sever a man automatically from the Body of the Church, as does schism, or heresy, or apostasy." (Mystici Corporis, par. 30; op. cit., p. 19) He goes on to point out how faith and hope may be preserved in a soul which is deprived of charity and, therefore, of the divine life of grace. (Cf. S.Th., 2ᵃ 2ᵃᵉ,4,3–4, on the relation between faith and charity, and also on the nature of dead faith.)

Nevertheless, no matter how frequently such an anomaly may occur, it is always a monstrous thing. The monstrosity consists in this, that a person who has been embodied into Christ acts *as though* he were not a member of Christ's body. He does not permit the witness of love to flow, as it normally should, from the gifts of God—baptism and faith—which initially make him a member of the Church. This, however, does not make *the Church* less holy, for the defection from grace on the part of a member of the Church has as its cause that in him which belongs to the "old man." (Cf. Jas 1,13–18.)

As long as faith and hope remain such a person will doubtless be "illumined from above . . . [and] spurred on by the strong promptings of the Holy Spirit to salutary fear. . . ." (Mystici Corporis, ibid.; cf. Rom 6,1–11; St. Paul here parries the objection that if the grace of

Christ is as wonderful as he says it is, then members of Christ ought to "sin bravely" that grace may abound.) Surely the presence of sinners in the bosom of the Church is, far from being a scandal, at least to those who have the eyes of faith, rather a singular proof of the "catholicity," that is, the infinite largesse of the heart of Christ.

If, therefore, we think of the Church in terms of the new creation, without *specific* reference to the conditions of membership, then the new creature, that is, man rescued from the chaos of darkness, transferred into the kingdom of God's beloved Son, is a creature endowed with these divine gifts: (1) the baptismal character, a sign of the new covenant in Christ's blood, which is a pledge of grace; (2) a faith which impels him to witness or confess the love of God made manifest in Christ; (3) a disposition whereby his activity within the Church is ruled by or subjected to the authorities whose power comes from the new Law, that is, the grace of the Holy Spirit. (Cf. *S.Th.*, 1ᵃ 2ᵃᵉ,106,1, on the "new Law," whether or not it is written down.) Finally, this new creature, provided that he is living in accord with this new Law, is possessed of the Holy Spirit who dwells in the Church as a whole, and is the force from which proceeds every action that belongs truly to the Church.

Extra Ecclesiam Nulla Salus

The apparently uncompromising character of this formula, which has dogmatic force in the history of Christian tradition, has often been a scandal to non-Catholics, as well as a source of misunderstanding to Catholics. The former sometimes take it as a sign of the arrogance of Catholic authoritarianism. It has happened, on occasion, that ill-informed Catholics have, in fact, understood it arrogantly.

Therefore, in order to avoid any scandal or misunderstanding, it seems appropriate that we go back in history to a period when the formula could be set forth with no "apologetical bias." Actually this means examining the Scriptures, the source of apostolic tradition, to see what Christ and the apostles taught concerning membership in the Church as a *necessary means* of salvation. In making this examination it will become evident that no distinction is being made between "membership in the Church" and "incorporation into Christ," simply because such a distinction is entirely alien to the tradition of the Church. After this summary of the evangelical basis for the axiom, we shall add some precisions made by the Church in her authentic interpretation of tradition; finally we shall apply the axiom, insofar as possible, to the present situation.

If any scriptural text can be cited as the foundation for the axiom, it is St. Peter's courageous witness, made when he was put on trial for having preached Christ:

> This is "the stone that was rejected by you, the builders, which has become the corner stone." Neither is there salvation in any other. For there is no other name under heaven given to men by which we must be saved. (Ac 4,11–12)

No pope, council, or theologian has ever stated the case in terms stronger than these. St. Peter's witness, however, must be understood in the light of several precisions made in the Scriptures themselves.

First of all, we must take into account these words from St. John's gospel: "The light has come into the world, yet *men have loved the darkness* rather than the light, for their works were evil." (Jn 3,19) This shows conclusively that the axiom, *extra ecclesiam . . .* is to be understood of those men, and only them, to whom the light of God's revelation, made in Jesus Christ, has actually shone, and who have "loved the darkness," that is, have consciously refused to be illumined.

Second, it is equally certain that the axiom, whether expressed in Petrine language or in the terminology of the Fathers or of the Church's later dogmatic formulas (cf. Origen, *Homily on the Book of Joshua,* III,5 [*PG* 12,841f]; St. Cyprian, *Letter to Jubaianus on the Baptizing of Heretics,* c. 21 [*PL* 3,1123]; profession of faith demanded of the Waldensians by Pope Innocent III [D430]; statement of the universal power of the Roman Pontiff in the bull, *Unam Sanctam,* of Boniface VIII [D469]) is in no way a cover for sinful members of the Church. In other words, membership in the visible society of the Catholic Church is not a guarantee of salvation. In order that it be *salutary,* the faith which is professed by Catholics must be, in St. Paul's words, the "faith which works through charity." (Gal 5,6)

Finally, and this is a sort of corollary of the first evangelical precision, the axiom does not preclude a salutary relation to Christ and the Church which is latent or hidden. This we may infer from the incident related in the gospel according to St. Mark (9,37–40), in which our

Lord states that "no one who shall work a miracle in my name [shall] forthwith be able to speak ill of me. For he who is not against you is for you."

All that we can say to make more explicit the distinctions which seem to be present in the sources of the Church's dogma can be put into three categories: (1) the presentation and possible rejection of the light that is in the world; (2) the nature of the faith which is required on the part of a person to whom this light is revealed; (3) the nature of the possible hidden relation to Christ and the Church.

The ordinary way in which the light of Christ is presented to the world is, of course, the preaching of the gospel by someone to whom this sublime office is committed. We shall see later the precise character of this apostolic function, but now it is enough to say that this mission is committed to the Catholic Church. It follows from this that when the opportunity is given to listen to the gospel, a person is in a crucial situation. St. Luke's rather terse statement concerning the situation in Rome when St. Paul first arrived there to preach is illustrative: "Some believed what was said; and some disbelieved." (Ac 28,24) Those who disbelieved had no more excuse than did the Jews to whom Christ himself spoke. (Cf. Jn 8,45ff.) Their "ignorance," that is, their disbelief was culpable or vincible.

Still we can conceive of a situation, and doubtless it is verified in many cases, in which the ignorance of the gospel message is invincible. The reasons for the impossibility of overcoming this lack of knowledge can also be many—and we shall have something to say about them in speaking of our separated brothers—but the point at issue here is that the axiom, *extra ecclesiam* . . . , must be understood in connection with those who are subject to this "invincible ignorance." The most authoritative statements of the Catholic doctrine on this point are those made by Pope Pius IX, remarkably enough, in two documents in which he explicitly treated the error of *indifferentism* (the allocution, *Singulari quadam,* Dec. 9, 1845 [D1647], and the encyclical letter *Quanto conficiamur moerore,* Aug. 10, 1863 [D1677]).[2] The pope says quite clearly

---

[2] See also this same pope's letter, written to Protestants on the occasion of the convocation of the first Vatican Council, *Iam vos omnes,* 13 Sept., 1868, ASS, 4, 131-35. The Holy Father is quite forthright in denying the "branch theory," according to which certain non-Catholic Christian communions would be considered as "collective members" or parts of the Catholic Church.

that those who are invincibly ignorant of the true religion, who, more-over, obey the precepts of the natural law, and who, while leading a good life, are ready to obey God (cf. Rom 1,5, where St. Paul speaks of the "obedience to faith"), can, in virtue of divine light and grace, attain eternal life.

This introduces us quite naturally to the second point, the nature of the faith which is required on the part of even those who are invincibly ignorant of the gospel. We can conclude, first of all, even from the statements of Pius IX, that it is supernatural faith that is in question, because he speaks of "divine light and grace." Theologians cite in this context the words of Hebrews: ". . . without faith it is *impossible* to please God." (Heb 11,5b)

A further question, however, is suggested by the phrase which follows immediately: "For he who comes to God must believe that God exists and is a rewarder to those who seek him." (*Ibid.*, 6) The question is, precisely what is the content of the faith spoken of here? Does "God" mean the triune God? And does this also imply a supernatural knowledge of the mystery of the incarnation of the Word of God?

Theologians have answered these questions somewhat differently in the course of the centuries, and one of the factors in the development of thought on the matter seems to have been the discovery, at the end of the fifteenth century, that there were vast numbers of human beings who could never possibly have heard of the incarnation or of the Trinity of persons, but some of whom appeared to have worshipped God "in spirit and in truth." St. Thomas' own discussion of the problem centers around the question of the mystery of Christ. Speaking of the present dispensation he says that ". . . everyone is held to have an explicit faith concerning the mysteries of Christ—especially those which are celebrated commonly in the Church, and are publicly proclaimed" (2^a 2^{ae},2,7; cf. art. 8.) Other theologians are of the opinion that it is possible to make a valid comparison between those who lived before the coming of Christ, at which time most people did not have an explicit knowledge of the mystery of Yahweh's love, and the nations who have not heard the gospel preached. In this case the words of St. Paul, "that God exists and is a rewarder of those who seek him," might be interpreted to mean that the supernatural faith required of those who are invincibly ignorant of the gospel is directed toward God—the supreme Being who rules over the universe, whose wise providence extends to every part of it, and whose special care is for his children, the members of the human race.

There is, however, another mystery to be found in this conclusion, because of its nature, living faith inclines a person to desire to conform with all that God, in his wisdom, prescribes for believers. What then, is the relationship of such believers to Christ and his Church? The answer to this question seems to be contained in *Mystici Corporis*. "Unsuspectingly," says Pius XII, "they are related in desire and resolution [*voto et desiderio . . . ordinantur*] to the mystical body of the Redeemer." It is, after all, the grace of Christ, and the breath of his Spirit, which have caused in them what is normally the result of a sacramental contact with our Lord (although the character of the sacrament cannot be present except by baptism of water.) In other words, they implicitly tend toward membership in the mystical body, the Church. And this is possible simply because Christ, the author of the Church, and his Spirit, her soul, together transcend the visible channels in which the grace of Christ ordinarily flows. This is not to say that the conditions of membership are accidental to the Church as such. Far from it, they are established in the will of Christ himself, made abundantly clear in the apostolic tradition. It does, however, mean that Christ is not "bound by the sacraments." As his bride, the Church cannot but obey him. She must preach the gospel to all nations; she is impelled to do so for love of Christ—her spouse. Yet she knows that she has other children who do not know her, but who are "destined together with us to eternal salvation, [though] not yet joined [to] us in the Body of the Church." (*Mystici Corporis,* par. 113; *op. cit.,* p. 46)

The magisterium of the Church has, to be sure, made certain pronouncements concerning the mystery of membership, and this teaching is a guide to a theological expression of the mystery. It is still true that a perfect way of expressing this complexus of truths—to include all the possible relations to the Church—is a work that the theologians of the Church are engaged in at present.

SEPARATED CHRISTIANS AND THE CHURCH

At the present time, there is perhaps the possibility that the Church's mission be extended farther than ever before. Nevertheless, *43* it is certain that some nations have not yet heard the gospel preached.

The situation of these pagan peoples can, it appears, be grasped in light of the principles we have just discussed.

There is, however, at least one problem which seems to be more difficult, and that is the vast number of Christians (principally the Orthodox and the Protestants) who are separated from the visible Church. The question invariably arises, what precisely is their relation to the Church?

The presumption we shall use as a basis for discussing this problem is that the vast majority of Orthodox and Protestant Christians today answer to St. Augustine's description of those who defend a position that is in some way false. They do not do so obstinately; instead, their position is one which has been inherited from preceding generations. In other words, they are "dissidents in good faith." Perhaps it ought to be said that this presumptive judgment is based on criteria altogether exterior; no man can know in a particular case what the state of a soul is.

What we see, therefore, in the Orthodox Churches is a people living a sacramental life under the direction of a hierarchy whose origins in the apostolic succession are unquestioned. Baptism is, of course, administered; the eucharist and other sacraments are celebrated. All this is in the Catholic tradition; but we see other things which are regrettable. Chief among these is the misunderstanding which the Orthodox have of the position of the pope in the Church. There are two results of this misunderstanding: (1) the primacy of Peter's successor, an article of Catholic faith, is denied (together with his infallibility); (2) submission to him is refused. Thus, materially, the Orthodox, though possessed of many elements of membership in the Church, are divided in faith and government.

The situation of the Protestant Christian community is, of course, much more complex.[3] The principles of the Reformation are such that we may be certain that there is lacking any real succession of the apostolic ministry. Still, for reasons that are evident from the theology of the sacrament of baptism, this sacrament may be and doubtless is validly administered in many Protestant communions. Consequently, where two baptized Protestants contract the bond of matrimony, the sacrament of marriage is validly received. Besides this, many if not most of the truths

44

---

[3] We include here, with certain reservations, the Anglican Communion which is, in the United States, the Protestant Episcopal Church.

of the Catholic faith are preached from Protestant pulpits, and upon these truths our separated brothers are nurtured in faith. Yet, and this is the tragedy of the situation, the misunderstanding of the mystery of the Church is such that these same Christians oppose the Roman Catholic Church. They are divided from her in faith and government, not, we may presume, in a formally heretical or schismatic way, but because of their inheritance of a tradition that was first altered in the sixteenth century.

If we consider the words of Pius XII in *Mystici Corporis* concerning the relation to the mystical body of the Redeemer "by desire and resolution," it seems that we must conclude that this relation on the part of dissident Christians is very intimate, much more so than is that of those who have not come into any sacramental contact with Christ, or who have not heard preached any of the elements of the Catholic faith.

It is in this light that we must judge the value of the "ecumenical movement" in which great segments of the Orthodox and Protestant communities are engaged. This movement, which is rooted historically in the missionary endeavors of the various Protestant communions, aspires toward a Catholic unity, unsuspectingly, perhaps, and by desire and resolution.

Today it is widely recognized that there is a special apostolate or mission which may be called "Catholic ecumenism." The *magna charta* of this mission is the *Instruction of the Holy Office,* issued on Dec. 20, 1949.[4] In this instruction it is stated clearly that the "ecumenical movement," that is, the efforts made on the part of non-Catholic Christians to discover Catholic unity, is an effect of the "inspiring grace of God." For this reason, certain provisions are made whereby the Catholic Church, that is to say, all Catholics under the leadership and the guidance of the bishops or shepherds of the flock, may meet this challenge or engage in this mission.

This is a mission, first of all, of love and sympathy, which should lead to understanding. On the basis of this understanding it is suggested that theological discussions ("dialogues") are possible and feasible, where the hope of good results is well founded. What are these "good results"?

45

---

[4] An English translation of this instruction is published by the Graymoor Press, Peekskill, N.Y., as the first number of a series called "Unity Studies."

Ultimately, of course, the good result which Catholic ecumenism, as a special mission or apostolate intends, is the common good of the Church: the perfect integration of all separated Christians into the one Church of Christ. This does not mean, however, that a "conversion" is always the immediate object of an ecumenical dialogue. The mission is preparatory. Furthermore, if we consider the "catholic capacity" of the Church to embrace all things, rooted in the espousals of the Church and Christ, it is possible to conclude that the reintegration of non-Catholic Christians into Catholic unity will cause the beauty of the Church to be multiplied. In other words, reintegration does not mean an absolute suppression of everything which might apparently be distinctive of Orthodoxy or Protestantism. Rather it means the purification of that which is a mixture of good and bad, all for the greater glory of Christ and *his* Church. This is allied to the continual purification which the Church must engage in with respect to her own understanding of her faith and its exercise.

It seems of particular interest to laymen in the Church that the differences which separate Catholic and non-Catholic are by no means all theological in nature. Catholicity, Orthodoxy, and Protestantism are all more than sets of beliefs. Each of them is a separate culture; the creed in each case is the root of its sociological, political, and economic features. These elements should be carefully distinguished from each other. The layman, perhaps, is in a better position to do this than the cleric. This is the reason we say that ecumenism is a mission of the Church as a whole. The part each member of the Church has to play should become clearer from our subsequent study of the various functions of members of the Church.

This rather lengthy discussion of the axiom *extra ecclesiam nulla salus* can be brought to a close with a reference to another document of the Holy Office, a letter written in 1949 to Cardinal Cushing (then Archbishop) and made public in 1952. (Cf. Appendix II of C. J. Dumont's *Approaches to Christian Unity* [Baltimore: Helicon, 1959, pp. 224ff]). In this letter the sense of the axiom is summed up as follows:

(1) Christ gave a strict command to the apostles to preach the gospel to all nations.

(2) Among those things to be preached was an invitation to be incorporated into the Church, the body of Christ,

by baptism and to abide in the Church by adhering to the Vicar of Christ, St. Peter's successor.

(3) Therefore, anyone who knows the Catholic Church to be of divine institution, and, nonetheless, refuses to submit to her authority, cannot be saved.

(4) Since, however, membership in the Church, as a condition of attaining eternal life, is not of intrinsic necessity, but of positive though divine institution, the end for which the Church was instituted may also, in certain extraordinary circumstances, be attained when the condition is fulfilled only by "desire or resolution." (Cf. *Mystici Corporis, ut supra.*)

(5) Sometimes this desire may be implicit.

These points are no more than a homogeneous development of what we have seen to be contained in germ in the gospels, that is, in the preaching of Christ and the apostles.

RELIGIOUS LIFE IN THE CHURCH

The terms in which we have explained the conditions of membership in the Church indicate, of themselves, that such incorporation into the body of Christ is not a final goal. Baptism is a door; profession of faith is an open witnessing to divine truth; and obedience to ecclesiastical authority is designed to form the visible body of Christ into the Perfect Man. In a word, all these elements are ordered to the perfection of the love of God in each of the members of the Church, and to that perfection of fraternal charity shared by all, whose effect must be the consummation of the unity of the Church.

Thus, if we presuppose the basic distinction according to which the Church as a whole is separated from the "world" (even though her mission never ceases to be universal), it is possible—and necessary—to make other distinctions. Some will be based upon the very nature of Christian or ecclesial perfection; others will have their origin in the dispositions made by Christ himself to insure the beauty of his bride.

The first distinction, therefore, among members of the Church has as its foundation charity or the love of God. In other words, members

47

of the Church are distinguished according to the degree of their conformity to Christ's new commandment (Jn 13,34f), since Christian perfection and the twofold love of God and neighbor are synonymous. (Cf. *S.Th.*, 2ª 2ᵃᵉ,184,1.) Furthermore, it is traditional that this distinction be articulated in terms of the "three ways": (1) the way of "beginners"; (2) that of "proficients"; (3) the way of the "perfect." (Cf. *S.Th.*, 2ª 2ᵃᵉ,183,4.)

Such a distinction among the members of the Church is of course fundamentally interior and invisible. The degree to which a member of Christ has managed, through grace, to divest himself of affection for created goods in order to adhere more perfectly to God, the common good of the Church, is fundamentally imperceptible. Still, to introduce this distinction is not superfluous; it is necessary for at least two reasons: (1) it draws our attention to the importance of the interior unity of the Church, the principle of which is the Holy Spirit, whose primary effect is charity (cf. Rom 5,5); (2) it shows us that so-called "spiritual theology" is intimately associated with the theology of the Church. The perfection of an individual member of Christ which is not related to the perfection of the whole body is absolutely inconceivable. (Cf. 1 Cor 12,25f.) The station in the Church that requires first mention is, of course, priesthood. No member of Christ is given such responsibilities with respect to the sacramental and the mystical body of Christ; the divine aid that priests receive is unique because their role in the Church is unique.

There is another aspect of this dynamic formation of the Church which is equally exterior and visible as priesthood—that state of perfection called the "religious life." In the mystical body the religious are members whose vocation includes precisely the witness to that plenitude of perfection toward which the whole Church tends. This "witness to perfection" given through a personal consecration to the acquiring of perfect charity with the help of certain means, ought to be an example to all other members of the Church.

First, it should be understood that the religious state is but an intensification of the Christian life as such. The basic perfection toward which religious (religious priests, brothers, and sisters or nuns) tend in the Church is in no way distinct from that which is the common goal of all members of the Church: the perfection of charity.

The distinctive character of the religious state, therefore, is derived

48

not from the end toward which religious in the Church tend, but rather from the means which are adopted by them, with the sanction of the Church herself, in order to remove what ordinarily impedes perfect love. These means, in general, are a sort of systematic exercise of the virtue of religion; in other words, the complete consecration of a person's life in the Church to the worship of God. The celebration of the Church's liturgy is essential to religious life, for what is done by lay people and their clergy in "the world" ought to be done by religious congregations with special fervor and solemnity.

Theologians sometimes speak of religious profession as a *holocaust*, that is, a complete sacrifice of the person for the honor of God. (Cf. *S.Th.*, 2ᵃ 2ᵃᵉ,186,1.) This holocaust is made concrete especially through the three vows of poverty, chastity, and obedience. Certain "monastic observances," which include manual labor and/or study, silence, and, to one degree or another, a common life, also contribute to its solidarity. This latter, however, takes on several different forms.

All these means have as their immediate purpose the removal of things which may impede to some degree the pursuit of Christian or ecclesial perfection. Put in a more positive way, each of the means which are essential to the religious life is designed to aid the religious in developing a virtue which will lay the groundwork of this perfection.

Although the members of all the various religious orders and congregations tend toward the perfection of charity, and this in common with all members of the Church, each of these same groups has something peculiar about it. That which is specific to each form of religious life in the Church is derived from what we may call "secondary" ends, namely specific goals which are subordinate to the perfection of charity. These secondary ends are the works of charity, that is, the activities which flow from the love of God and neighbor conceived in a spirit of contemplation.

Among those "traditions" which seem to be of apostolic origin, one seems to be the religious state. We can see in the New Testament certain indications of a special call made to some members of the Church to bear special witness to the perfection to which all are called. (Cf. Mt 19,10ff; Lk 18,18–30; 1 Cor 7,25–35.) In any case, it is certain that during the times which were immediately post-apostolic, men and women conscientiously began to live according to the evangelical counsels, and that the present panoply of religious orders in the Church is a homogeneous manifestation of that first *élan*. Most of them are present in the Church and exist for the Church—as "corporate members"—in order that Christ himself may accomplish his design, to manifest his Church "in all her glory, not having spot or wrinkle or any such thing, but that she might be holy and without blemish." (Eph 5,27)

CHAPTER FIVE

SPIRITUAL OFFICES
IN THE CHURCH

Up to the present we have been concerned with order and distinction in the Church and how they relate to the goal toward which the Church tends: the summing up, or recapitulation, of all things in him. Every degree of perfection in the Church, whether it be the inner holiness of the Church's members or an exterior witness to the sublimity of the Christian vocation—which seems to be an integral part of the role to be played in the Church by those called to the religious state—is a share in that final perfection which God intends for the bride of his beloved Son. These distinctions have something eschatological about them, in the sense that they foreshadow the perfection and beauty of the new Jerusalem, even though here and now the picture is obscure and incomplete. This is owing both to the presence of sinners in the Church and to the fact that the perfection of many of her members is hidden from the eyes of men.

Now, however, we shall consider briefly another kind of ecclesial order or distinction, the basis of which is more proximate to the Church's present life. Knowing by faith that the Church is a mystical person, all of whose members have something to contribute to her life, we can conclude that these members will be distinguished one from another not only with respect to the perfection of love to which all are called, but also according to the acts or functions which the various members have in the body of the Church. Furthermore, we shall call this latter order or distinction an order of spiritual power or office, because in every case where there is a special act or function, it is derived from some power. It is, moreover, scarcely necessary to observe that these spiritual powers are themselves derived from Christ, the author of the new creation. Besides being possessed of all the perfection of his body, the Church, he is also the font of every power exercised within it.

Also, by way of introduction, it might be observed that this consideration is, perforce, general and schematic. What is involved here, at least in part, is a doctrine of the function of lay people in the Church: a doctrine much discussed, the conclusions of which need much serious study and elaboration.[1]

The first thing, therefore, that we should like to establish is the most general distinction in this order of act or function in the Church. Again it is possible to have recourse to the epistles of St. Paul in order to see the basis of this general distinction. At the end of one disquisition concerning the Church as Christ's body, the apostle asks several pointed questions: "Are all apostles? Are all prophets? Are all teachers?" (1 Cor 12,29) Then, as if in answer to them, but in a different epistle, he affirms: "[Christ] gave some men as apostles, others again as evangelists, and others as pastors and teachers. . . ." (Eph 4,11)

---

[1] Consult the reading list proper to this chapter for some suggestions for further investigation.

Now in the history of the Church, the ecumenical council which was most concerned with the meaning that underlies these apostolic formulae was that of Trent. This council dealt with errors which had been propagated by the reformers of the sixteenth century; among these were several concerning the nature of the Church. One decree of that council, even though it was formulated in that peculiar context, seems to be the key to the distinction in question here: "If anyone should say that there is not, in the Catholic Church, a hierarchy, divinely instituted, which is composed of bishops, priests, and other ministers, let him be anathema." (Session XXIII, 15 July, 1563; can. 6[D966].

The significance of this decree, as far as we are concerned, is simply that within the Church the members are distinguished as either belonging or not belonging to the "hierarchy." We might even say that the Church *is* hierarchical; but this statement must be understood thoroughly. A better formulation would seem to be that, as far as the various ecclesial functions are concerned, some are exercised by a special group —bishops, priests, and other ministers—while others are proper to another group of members, which we call the laity. All these functions are ecclesial, but not all are hierarchical, and this by divine institution. In other words, the council is affirming that the distinction of function in the Church, which is the object of St. Paul's references, has been propagated through our time. With regard to those functions which are hierarchical, we shall see later that this distinction is based upon the apostolic succession.

For the present, however, we are more interested in determining a little more carefully the nature of the functions which are hierarchical and lay, respectively. Limiting ourselves still to a general statement, we shall say that the distinction consists in the following: spiritual powers which are possessed by members of the Church belonging to the hierarchy are ordered to the transmission or *giving* of holy things; the spiritual powers proper to the laity, however, are ordered to the *receiving* of holy things. One might say that the relation is one of active and passive principles to one another. Yet the foregoing distinction must be understood well. Notice that when we use the word "passive" to refer to the function of the laity in connection with the "holy things" in question, the term is coupled with another, namely "principle." This means that the act or function of receiving "holy things"—*what they are in particular is yet to be determined*—is itself rooted in a *real power to do.*

53

The laity in the Church, and especially in relation to the hierarchy, is not purely passive, even though the proper acts or functions are based upon a passive power. In other words this power is no less real than are the spiritual powers in which are rooted hierarchical functions, although it is of a different order.

Since Christ, Wisdom incarnate, is as we have seen the exemplar according to which the new creation is fashioned, any further delineation of the various functions in the Church, whether hierarchical or lay, must be based on what might be called the "functions of Christ himself." To the question, what are these functions, Catholic tradition gives a definite answer. The acts of the God-man in the founding and nourishing of his Church are rooted in his possession of a threefold dignity: prophetic, priestly, and royal.

Christ is the prophet or teacher *par excellence.* The Church has always been conscious that our Lord is the new Moses (cf. Dt 18,18; Jn 1,17), who comes to fulfill the Law and all the prophets. (Mt 5,17; cf. Lk 24,27.44f.) That he is the priest of the new Law is incontestable (cf. Heb 5,1–10); that he is king of the messianic domain is evident from the biblical images we have already discussed. Therefore, the functions both of the hierarchy and the laity may be more accurately determined under the sign of these three categories. In each case it will be a question of seeing how this or that dignity is shared, either in the order of transmitting, or again in the order of receiving. We can see from the outset that the "holy things" which are the objects of ecclesial acts or functions will be the *truth* implied by prophecy, the *grace* communicated through the priesthood, and the *rule* or government proper to royal power.

THE PROPHETIC FUNCTION
IN THE CHURCH

The meaning of this term in the present context must, first of all, be described. In this connection, two possible meanings can immediately be discarded. One is the concept of the "prophet" as it is developed in the Old Testament, that is, a man sent by God as a bearer of divine revelation to speak authentically to his chosen people Israel. This sort of prophecy was epitomized and consummated in Christ; in this sense, there are no more "public" prophets. Nor are we referring to the "prophets" of whom St. Paul speaks in the texts cited above, namely members of the Church endowed with extraordinary gifts of foretelling the future or even of expounding the hidden meaning of events. We have no reason to believe that such gifts of prophecy have not always been and will not always be present in the Church. Their presence, however, whether in members of the hierarchy or lay people, cannot be the object of the scrutiny of theology, except insofar as "private revelations" come under the judgment of the Church in her conservation of the deposit of faith.

It is, then, this "deposit of faith" which is most of all in question when we speak now of the prophetic function of the Church. One of the conditions of membership in the Church is the "profession of the true faith." Within the Church, therefore, there must be a guarantee that this is possible.

Right now we are not concerned with analyzing the elements of this necessary function—that will be the subject of a later chapter. We are merely pointing out how the hierarchy and the laity are distinguished one from the other in this respect. Applying the general distinction already made, we must say that it is the function of the hierarchy to teach (that is, to transmit, to *give*) the deposit of faith, while the act proper to the laity is to believe, or *receive* it.

Several additional remarks are in order. First, it is obvious that members of the hierarchy are also believing members of the Church. In other words, it is only in virtue of their special power—which presupposes incorporation into the body of Christ as members—that they are able to function in this *active* way. Second, it should be observed how the notion of passivity is verified here in connection with the laity. The faith of *any* member of the Church is rooted in the authority of God as self-revealing. The content of this faith is received, as is the motive by which a person adheres to it, under the inspiration of divine grace. Furthermore, Christ has ordained that this reception be dependent upon the apostolic *kḗ'rygma* and *didachē'*, that is to say, upon the preaching of the gospel by authorized ministers and the explanation of it in the Church. Consequently, the act of faith is a distinctly personal act, and to this extent, "lay" function is not at all passive.

There is more to be said. When we note that the function of the laity is to believe actively, this is not to be understood as including the

55

public profession of faith, that is, an open witness to God's truth in the presence of a world that is hostile to it. We perceive that the active and passive aspects of the prophetic function *within* the Church are quite clearly delineated. It is clear, too, that when the Church faces the chaos of the world to be re-created, both hierarchy and laity must cooperate in presenting the gospel message. The members of the hierarchy are doubtless divinely commissioned to "preach the gospel to all nations," but the profession of true faith on the part of lay people is a real participation in this function.

Furthermore, within the Church there must be lay cooperation with the hierarchy in this respect. Although it is the prerogative of the bishop to preach the gospel (a prerogative commonly shared with his priests and sometimes other ministers), nevertheless, in a lay group such as the Confraternity of Christian Doctrine nonhierarchical members of the Church are given the job of catechizing and instructing those who are less well-informed about the truths of faith.

Finally, there is an area, rather difficult to define, in which the entire "believing Church" participates in the prophetic function of the hierarchy. We shall discuss this later in connection with the nature of the Church's power to teach. For our present purposes it is necessary to say only that the consensus or common accord of all the faithful upon matters of faith is one of the norms by which the hierarchy is guided in the propagation and the conservation of Catholic truth. In this sense, too, the active prophetic function of the hierarchy is complemented by the passive role of lay people.

PRIESTHOOD IN THE CHURCH

Among the several errors of the Protestant Reformation, the one that seemed most of all to undermine the nature of the Church was the doctrine of the "common priesthood of all believers." Even though we should like to present a theology of the Church free from all apologetical concern, it is necessary to consider the distinction of hierarchy and laity with that error in mind, for even today the priesthood in the Church is the object of much misunderstanding.

56   To begin with, we shall consider the significance of the priestly consecration of the entire Church, an idea which is altogether scriptural.

St. Peter states this quite emphatically: "Be you also as living stones built up, a spiritual house, a holy priesthood, to offer up spiritual sacrifices, acceptable to God by Jesus Christ." (1 Pt 2,5) The source of this idea, at least as far as St. Peter is concerned, is the manner in which the Church fulfills the messianic hopes of Israel. (Cf. Ex 19,6.) Christ, as *the* priest of the new covenant, consecrates the Church in virtue of his living union with her so that, by him, she is capable of offering to the Father "spiritual sacrifices."

We cannot help but note the relation of priesthood and sacrifice which are necessary to one another. The Church as a whole is endowed with a sacerdotal role; she, *therefore,* offers spiritual sacrifices. Yet we must point out that this priestly function of the Church in the world does not offer a basis for any hierarchical distinction *within* the Church. In order to make that distinction we must have recourse to other principles, holding at the same time, that the spiritual priesthood of members of the Church (which may be called a "priesthood of personal righteousness") is altogether real. (Cf. Y. M.-J. Congar, *Lay People in the Church,* p. 180.)

That there is a distinction of hierarchy and laity in the context of priesthood is based, then, upon another factor—the institution by Christ of a *sacramental* sacrifice to be offered in the Church. When we distinguish between spiritual and sacramental sacrifice, we have no intention of denying the spiritual end for which the sacramental sacrifice —the eucharist—has been instituted. It is merely a question of pointing out that *this* sacrifice, by divine institution, requires distinction in the Church. It requires a consecrating priest, who, by virtue of an active power which is hierarchical, is capable of celebrating the sacrifice. He can take the bread and wine offered by the Church, set them aside for holy use, consecrate them by the use of the eucharistic formula, and communicate these consecrated things to the faithful.

This capacity is hierarchical in that it is derived from the consecration of the priest himself, through the sacrament of orders. As the Council of Trent teaches, such a member of the Church has received the Holy Ghost in a special way; his soul has been marked with a spiritual seal called the "character" of the sacrament of orders (cf. Session XXIII, 15 July, 1563; can. 4 [D964]). It is this consecration which distinguishes him from the laity.

Again, however, we must add certain remarks about the relation of the consecrated and consecrating priesthood in the Church to the laity, even in connection with the sacramental sacrifice of the Church. It would appear at first glance that the priesthood of the laity is restricted to that common "priesthood of personal righteousness" mentioned above. This, however, is not true. Even in the sacramental sacrifice—perhaps above all in it—the laity has a function. True, its members are "receivers," but, again, they are *consecrated* to receive. They are also endowed with a power, in this case a power to participate, in the eucharistic sacrifice of the Church.

This important subject of the participation of the laity in the Church's sacrifice—to which we shall refer in discussing the Church's return to Christ through love—may be elucidated in two different ways. The first is negatively, for according to Pius XII, "that the faithful participate in the Eucharistic Sacrifice, does not mean that they are also endowed with priestly power." (The encyclical letter on the Sacred Liturgy [*Mediator Dei*] [Vatican Library Translation, NCWC], par. 82, p. 32.) This much is clear: there is a distinction. From a positive point of view, much is left to be said—and more to be done.

In the first place, the Holy Father in this same letter indicates that the power to participate is based upon the spiritual seal or character imprinted upon the soul of every Christian in baptism. (*Ibid.*, par. 88, p. 34) Then he goes on to enumerate two ways in which this capacity is activated: (1) inasmuch as the people make the offering of the bread and wine to be used in the sacrifice; (2) insofar as when, through the consecrating priest, Christ becomes present upon the altar, the laity participate in the offering of this oblation "for the glory of the blessed Trinity and for the good of the whole Church." (*Ibid.*, par. 92, p. 35)

In summary fashion, therefore, we can list the following points as regulative of the order or distinction of hierarchy and laity with respect to priesthood:

(a) the general distinction of giving and receiving is verified in virtue of the sacerdotal character imprinted upon the souls of priests in the sacrament of orders;

(b) all of the faithful through incorporation into Christ form a "holy priesthood" whose act is "spiritual sacrifice," that is, a life in accord with the gospel;

58 (c) this same incorporation, which is accomplished especially through baptism, enables the faithful to participate actively in the sacra-

mental sacrifice of the eucharist, the minister being the consecrating priest.

ROYALTY IN THE CHURCH

The third and last aspect of this distinction is concerned with the function of rule or government. Before anything else, special attention should be paid to the character of ecclesial rule. Its motif was indicated once and for all by our Lord in the cenacle. Christ, observing that his apostles were wrangling over who was to be the greatest among them, gave them a rule which regulates all *exercise* of royal power in the Church. "Let him who is greatest among you become as the youngest, and him who is the chief as the servant." (Lk 22,26; the account of the entire episode should be read.)

Granting, however, that in the Church no one is to "lord it over" anyone else, because even the sovereign King is in the Church "as one who serves," still even from this passage we can infer that there must be a distinction of rule or government. The ruler is, to be sure, a minister; he is to give his life for his flock. The pope calls himself *servus servorum Dei*, originally a genitive of intensity meaning chief servant, but in Western speech understood as one who serves others who serve. Nevertheless the authority which the pope or anyone else in the Church exercises is a royal power, deriving from the plenitude of Christ's kingship.

In this respect again, the hierarchy is distinguished from the laity. The former actively govern the Church, Christ's body, while the laity are governed. Within the limits established by the institution of Christ, the members of the hierarchy have the right to the obedience of the faithful. These limits are set by the goal of the Church, that is to say the holiness of its members.

Since the next section of our study is to be concerned directly with the manner in which this rule is verified, we need not spell out here all the necessary distinctions. We should like to emphasize, however, that the orientation of the faithful toward the common good of the Church is accomplished through activity which is altogether intelligent and spontaneous. The Church as a mystical person is an organism in which the members do not lose their personal autonomy. On the con-

59

trary, incorporation into Christ and growth in him enhances everything that is truly human. Besides this, we should remark that the laity share in Christ's royalty *vis à vis* the world. The Church is a society of royal people because each and every member is in living union with the King of Kings. It is in this sense that we may understand the words of St. Paul: "Do you not know that the saints will judge the world? . . . Do you not know that we shall judge angels? How much more worldly things!" (1 Cor 6,2f)

Starting, in this section, with the biblical images of the Church, we have elaborated what seem to be the principal distinctions through which the Church receives her order. We have seen that as *Christ's* kingdom she is separated or distinguished radically from the kingdom of evil. Furthermore we have seen that within the kingdom there are other distinctions, all of which contribute in some way to the perfection, the beauty, and the activity of the Church. With regard to perfection and beauty we have discussed not only the conditions of membership but also the panoply of perfection, interior and exterior, which is exhibited by the various members. Finally, we have tried to show that all the activity in which the Church must engage as a living supernatural organism is articulated through the different functions of hierarchy and laity; all are exercised in dependence upon Christ—Prophet, Priest, and King. "For from him the whole body (being closely joined and knit together through every joint of the system according to the functioning in due measure of each single part) derives its increase to the building up of itself in love." (Eph 4,16)

CHAPTER SIX

THE PRINCIPLE
OF MEDIATION

In shifting our attention from the order which Christ the incarnate Wisdom has given to the new creation, our concern in Chs. 3, 4, and 5, to the governing of it, which shall be the work of Chs. 6 and 7, we are making an important transition. (Cf. the opening remarks of Ch. 3, p. 21.) Even though membership in the Church, like the various functions of different members, suggests growth and activity, the whole emphasis of our approach has been upon a static articulation. This emphasis needs to be complemented by a more explicit consideration of the principles by which the Church is actually led to that perfection for which she has been created. In other words, we need to direct our attention to the manner in which this mystical person is enabled, more and more perfectly, to reflect him in whose image she has been created, namely Christ. This consideration will lead naturally into the second part of our study, which will concern the *activity* of the Church. It is to be noted, from the outset, that the principles of the Church's government are also the work of Wisdom.

The most fundamental reason that can be adduced to account for this aspect of the mystery of the Church is suggested by St. Thomas Aquinas in his treatment of God's providence. The question arises in the context of whether or not God provides *immediately* for all things that he has created. The distinction which Aquinas employs here is one that can be applied both to the natural and the supernatural orders. He observes, first of all, that two aspects of God's providence must be taken into account: (1) the *conception* of the order of created realities with respect to the ends provided for them in their very creation; (2) the *execution* of this order, which is properly called government. There is no question but that God conceives this order immediately, down to the slightest detail. The execution, however, takes place differently:

> Regarding this second aspect, there are certain means of divine providence. The inferior are governed through the superior, and this is not because of any defect in God's power, but rather on account of the abundance of his goodness. This is such that he communicates even to creatures the dignity of causality. (*S.Th.*, 1ª,22,3)

Now, the mystery of the redemptive incarnation is really the epitome of all the "means of God's providence." No doubt we can understand the words of St. Paul in this sense: "For there is one God, and one Mediator between God and men, himself man, Christ Jesus." (1 Tim 2,5) In other words if we consider the power of God alone, the plan for the new creation could have been otherwise. In his superabundant goodness, however, God ordained that the new creation should have as its head the new Adam (cf. Rom 5,15), and that the dignity of causality

62

in the supernatural order of grace should above all be communicated to him.

As head of the Church, therefore, Christ has absolute supremacy. There is a sense in which we must say that he is the unique mediator between God and men. It seems to have been the intent of the sixteenth century reformers to affirm this truth in such a way as to exalt Christ's mediation. This intent, however, was vitiated by the exclusiveness with which the principle was stated.

This mediation of Christ, the principle of all government, is altogether universal. No element of the new creation is exempt from his influence. This is just another way of saying what we have already said, that there is perfect identity between the Church and Christ's mystical body.

This unique mediation of Christ, however, ought not to be understood in an exclusive sense. Even though St. Thomas asserts quite forcefully that to be a mediator between God and men belongs properly to Christ as man, he does not shrink from adding: "Nothing, however, prohibits some others from being, in a certain fashion (*secundum quid*), mediators between God and men, according as they cooperate to join men with God, either by disposing them properly or as ministers." (*S.Th.*, 3ᵃ,26,1c)

What this statement means can be made clear if we return to the idea of Christ as the author of the new creation. Surely the plan of this new creation belongs, under God, to Christ even or indeed especially in his manhood. His infinite love for the Church for which he delivered himself proceeds from a knowledge—and an effective knowledge—which is quite perfect, down to the last detail. This knowledge transcends time, so that our Lord is able to see the Church militant in relation to the perfection for which she is destined. We might call this knowledge "Christ's providence for the new creation."

What, then, of the execution of this eminently perfect practical wisdom? Does Christ exercise it alone? Does he, in his sacred humanity, guard for himself the prerogative of bringing to perfection, that is, to its end, the Church he has created? No doubt he could. There is no limit, absolutely speaking, to his power. But does he? No, he does not. Paraphrasing St. Thomas we answer: "On account of the superabundance of his goodness and love he communicates even to creatures—in the new creation—the dignity of causality."

A single precision will complete this doctrine. It is evident that since this new creation, the Church, as a supernatural organism, the execution of Christ's designs, will be entirely in the order of grace. In other words, it is a share in God's life which is involved; therefore the first and proper cause of any and all effects in this order must be God himself. Even the sacred humanity of Christ himself is but an instrument. His human nature is, in the words of St. John Damascene, the "organ of divinity." Thus the communication of the dignity of causality to other mediators in the new creation must be in this line. "Let a man so account of us, as servants of Christ and stewards of the mysteries of God." (1 Cor 4,1) This is the way in which St. Paul suggests that all of the mediation in the Church, which is derived from the apostolic mission, is a ministry, a stewardship. All the glory belongs to Christ, and through him, to God.

Once again, it is possible to see here an application of the mystery of our Lady in the Church. We have observed before that, as far as her interior life is concerned, she is the most perfect image of Christ the exemplar of the new creation. Here, then, we have the opportunity of observing that Christ in his infinite love for his mother willed her to be associated with him most intimately in executing his plan for the Church. It is not within our province to discuss how this is verified in the mystery of the redemption. That pertains to the theology of the incarnate Word and of his work on earth. What we are interested in is our Lady's mediation in the Church of the graces won by Christ on Calvary.

Catholic tradition authorizes our affirming that this mediation of Mary is universal, in other words that it extends to the entire life of the Church. She has been called, by analogy with her Son, the "mediatrix of all graces." This is a point of doctrine not defined by the Church's *magisterium*, but it is her common teaching. Her privilege of mediation is rooted first in the consent she gave which made possible a "spiritual marriage between the Son of God and human nature," and second in her intimate union with Christ on Calvary, where "her mother's rights and mother's love were included in the holocaust" (Pius XII, *Mystici Corporis*, par. 130; *op. cit.*, p. 51). Finally it is rooted in her powerful intercession which "obtained the grace that the Spirit of our divine redeemer, already given to the Church on the cross, should be bestowed through miraculous gifts on the newly founded hierarchy on Pentecost."

64

The special reason for our including this consideration in a chapter which is designed to establish the general principles of mediation in the government of the Church is that our Lady's mediation transcends any particular effect of these principles. Her dignity is not hierarchical; she is not a priest. Even though the liturgy says that in her "is all grace of the way and of the truth" (Coh 24,25; lesson of the Mass for the Vigil of the Assumption), our Lady was never possessed of any mission to teach or to make laws in the Church. Her mediation in the Church and the queenship that she exercises in the kingdom of her Son are not visible, although in the new Jerusalem where she reigns even now we shall see that what the liturgy says of her is altogether true: "You are exalted, most holy Mother of God, above the choirs of angels in the heavenly kingdom."

CHAPTER SEVEN

EFFECTIVENESS OF CHURCH GOVERNMENT

So far the topic of the government of the Church, as it is a visible mystery, has been touched upon on two occasions. This has been done briefly and more or less obliquely. The first instance was in the chapter which dealt with the historical moments of the new creation. (Ch. 2) There Christ was seen as having chosen twelve apostles, and as having singled out from among them Simon to be the rock upon which he should build his Church. It is evident now, especially in light of the principles laid down in the immediately preceding chapter, that these choices of Christ were the source of a *ministry* in the Church, that is, of a transmission of spiritual powers. The second occasion was in the chapter on that distinction within the Church which is based upon "office." The point made there was simply that the members of the hierarchy, who derive their active power in one degree or other from the "apostolic succession," are placed in the Church in order to direct or to give the proper orientation to the movement of the Church.

The task of this chapter, therefore, is to give greater precision to our ideas about these directive or governing powers. The procedure that we shall follow is to be based upon that fundamental analogy according to which the Church is considered a new creation. The effects of God's government of the visible universe can be looked at from several points of view. First of all, the entire movement of the universe tends to be consummated in a marvelously various yet unified participation in, and likeness to, the divine good, for which all things have been created. It is also possible to consider these effects as to the ways in which this participation and likeness are accomplished. St. Thomas suggests that there are, from this second point of view, only two effects of the divine government.

> The creature is made like God in two ways, first, as regards God's goodness, insofar as the creature is *good*; second, as regards God's being the cause of goodness in others, insofar as one creature moves another toward goodness. Thus the two effects of divine government are: (1) conservation of things in their goodness; (2) their movement toward the good. (*S.Th.*, 1ª,103,4)

Here the Angelic Doctor notes that if divine government is considered as to its particular effects, since they are innumerable they cannot be subject to any scientific treatment.

In applying these ideas, therefore, to the Church as the new creation of which Christ is the author, we shall be interested in the two general effects which are, (1) conservation and (2) movement (*motio*). The first question, moreover, which demands an answer is: what *is* the "good" of the Church? This is important simply because both maintenance or conservation and movement are determined, as it were, by *goodness.*

Since the Church is the new creation, we must say, first of all, that her proper good is altogether distinct from the good or perfection of the natural universe. Her good is *super*natural. She is, by very definition, a supernatural organism, a mystical person whose head is Christ. On the other hand, we must say that the supernatural good proper to the Church is only a participation in and likeness of the divine goodness. In a word, the good of the Church, which is to be conserved and promoted by effective rule, is her union with God through the grace of Christ as shared by those who are incorporated into him. This good of the Church is, therefore, the *sanctity of her members*.

The holiness or sanctity of Yahweh, the God of Israel, is a theme which permeates the entire Old Testament. This is, as it were, his essential attribute. (Cf. Lv 11,44f; 19,2; 20,7.26; 21,8; 22,32f.) The prophet Isaia often calls him the "Holy One of Israel" (e.g. Is 1,4; 5,19.24; 10,17.20; 41,14.16.20.) It was in virtue of their having been chosen by the Lord as *his* people that the Israelites were a *holy* people. This holiness of Israel was to manifest itself especially by fidelity to the Law that had been given to them by God through the mediation of Moses. We can understand, therefore, the significance of the prophecy of Jeremia, in which he says: ". . . after those days, says the Lord, I will place my law within them, and write it upon their hearts; I will be their God, and they shall be my people." (Jer 31,33f)

The holiness of the Church, which is communicated to her members by Jesus Christ the new Moses (cf. Jn 1,17), is a new Law, "the entire force of which is the grace of the Holy Spirit, which is given through faith in Christ." (*S.Th.*, 1ª 2ᵃᵉ,106,1) Thus we see that the terms grace of Christ, new Law, and Christian holiness, are all different ways of expressing the same idea, namely the means through which are communicated to the Church those qualities which prepare her immediately for union with God. This is the effect which must be preserved and promoted in the Church: that the grace of Christ be more and more diffused in her; that the new Law be ever more perfectly promulgated; in a word, that her members fulfill their vocation to Christian holiness. "[God] chose us in [Christ] before the foundation of the world, that we should be holy and without blemish in his sight and love." (Eph 1,4) (Cf. 5,27b.)

68 Before we discuss more in particular these elements of the government of the Church—all oriented toward holiness as they are—there is

one other idea about the new Law which ought to be made clear. There is no doubt but that this Law and the invisible grace of the Holy Spirit which is given to those who believe in Christ are one and the same thing. St. Thomas, however, furnishes a remark which intimates that all along we shall be dealing with visible and tangible realities:

> The new Law is possessed of some elements which are *dispositive* in relation to the grace of the Holy Spirit, and which pertain to the use of this grace. They are, as it were, secondary elements of the new Law, concerning which it is necessary that Christ's faithful be instructed both by word of mouth and in writing. These have to do both with things to be believed, and with actions. Thus, one must affirm that whereas the new Law is primarily an infused Law, secondarily it is written. (*S.Th.*, 1ª 2ᵃᵉ,106,1)

This text is by no means conclusive proof that the Church's government is able to be seen and touched. It does, however, suggest that holiness depends on what is within sight and reach. These are the things in the Church's constitution which seem to be entirely human. If we approach them as such, however, we shall be missing one of the most important aspects of the mystery that God has given to creatures—the dignity of causing in part their own sanctification. In the new covenant of the grace of Christ, the holiness of the Church—her own proper good—is "hidden in Christ." This does not mean that this property of holiness cannot be discerned or that it is not, to a certain degree, evident to all. It does mean, however, that the means according to which it is communicated are visible and tangible and human. "Of *his* fullness we have all received," says St. John. (Jn 1,16) We must never forget that this fullness is the infinite grace of the God-*man*, Jesus Christ.

HOLINESS OF THE CHURCH THROUGH THE POWER OF ORDER

Paradoxically, in a place where he is speaking of the sin of schism, or the rupture of the unity of the Church by a refusal to take one's place in the order established by Christ, St. Thomas suggests how one might distinguish the conservation of the Church's holiness, itself a dynamic reality, from the means that renew it.

69

> Spiritual power is twofold: one is sacramental and the other is juris-
> dictional. Sacramental power is that power which is conferred by
> means of a consecration. Now all the consecrations of the Church
> "stand" so long as the thing which is consecrated continues in exist-
> ence. (*S.Th.*, 2ᵃ 2ᵃᵉ,39,3)

Now, therefore, we are going to discuss that spiritual power in the
Church which is sacramental, and which, by the will of Christ, is altogether indefectible.

We have said that what is involved is the holiness of the members
of the Church, in other words, their being possessed of that grace (a real
share in the most intimate life of God) which Christ possessed in its
fullness. The question is: how is this grace stabilized or continued in
the Church? Christ, the head of the Church, has removed himself from
this earth according to his physical presence. He will not return until
the Day of Judgment. Certainly he is always present to the Church;
but is there a manner in which he gives indefectible continuance to the
holiness of his bride—her dowry as it were?

The answer to this question, of course, is contained germinally
in the text cited above. It is by the sacramental power of orders, in other
words through the Christian priesthood, that the grace of Christ—the
good proper to the Church which makes her holy—is maintained and
nurtured. The reasons for this are evident from the principles of sacramental theology. Christ willed that his grace and holiness be communicated to his members through sacred signs called the sacraments. These
symbolic rites are sacraments of the Church. Administered in no other
society, they were instituted in order to increase the Church's holiness.
They are, according to the will of Christ, *her* property.

Furthermore, in the theology of the sacraments we learn that each
of these symbolic rites requires a *minister* who acts in the name of Christ,
the author of the sacraments; that is to say, in the name of the Church.
St. Thomas' point is that administering sacraments requires a consecration in virtue of which a man is given the power to be a minister for
Christ and in the Church. This is the first application of the principle
of mediation discussed in the previous chapter, and it ought to be
noted that this mediation is altogether peculiar. The minister of the
sacraments of Christ (and of the Church) is taken up so intimately into
Christ through the symbolic rite that he actually shares in that virtue
proper to the sacraments—to communicate holiness or grace. This does

not mean, of course, that he communicates his special grace or holiness to the person who shares in the sacramental rite; but rather that through him, as minister of the sacrament, the grace of Christ is conferred. In every case, it is by the words of the minister that the sacramental rite is given its form. "I baptize you, . . ."; "I confirm you, . . ."; "This is my body; this is the chalice of my blood, . . ."

Another conclusion which can be derived from what has been said is that the holiness of the Church, in her earthly existence, is a sacramental holiness. If, as we learn in the theology of the sacraments, each of these symbolic rites confers a share in the grace of Christ which is modified by the very sign under which it is given, then the entire marvelous life of the Church is determined by these "sacramental modes." It is the task of sacramental theology to distinguish what these modes are. We should like, however, to emphasize one point. Whereas Christ is not "bound to the sacraments" in the sense that he is free to communicate to a soul the life of grace without employing the sacraments, nevertheless, he has given them to the Church as part of the new Law. She is bound to them as she is bound to Christ, her spouse. In the prescriptions of love there is no bondage, properly speaking. There is only commitment and mutual fidelity in acts of love.

Among these sacramental rites is one that insures the conservation of all the rest: the sacrament of order. According to the dogma of the Church, Christ ordained that the twelve apostles be her first priests. Furthermore, he willed that this power of order be passed on in the Church, so that at no moment in history should she be deprived of the priesthood. This is surely one of the meanings of his promise: ". . . behold, I am with you all days, even unto the consummation of the world." (Mt 28,20) In a sense, the presence of the priesthood, here and now, is an absolute guarantee of the Church's holiness. This fact is an object of our faith, since both the proximate source of holiness and the holiness itself are sacramental; invisible grace is contained within visible symbols.

The way in which the priestly mediation of Christ is articulated in the Church has its prototype in the apostolic college. Peter's primacy was a *priestly* primacy. The other apostles were associated with him as high priests in the new Israel. We may take it as symbolic Christ's having appointed "seventy-two others" during his lifetime to assist the Twelve in the harvest of souls. Over the centuries the pope, bishop of

Rome and successor of St. Peter, is, as Pius XI said in an encyclical, "at the summit of the priesthood." The other bishops, although possessing the fullness of the priesthood in their own right, in virtue of their episcopal consecration, are nevertheless subordinate to the Church's first priest. A fortiori, the priests whose office is of second rank (such is the wording of the ordination rite) hold their place in the sacerdotal order of the Church as bishops' subordinate co-workers. This is true whether they belong to the secular or regular clergy.

It seems incumbent upon lay people to be acutely aware of the function of the priesthood to propagate and nourish the holiness of Christ's mystical body. On this vocation is based the law of the Church which reads: "Clerics ought to lead an interior and exterior life that is holier than that of lay people, as well as to edify them by virtue and good deeds." (CIC 124; cf. the encyclical of Pius XII, Menti Nostrae, on the development of holiness in priestly life; in translation, Washington: NCWC, 1950.) This obligation rests first of all on the shoulders of priests themselves; they are called to holiness because they are ministers of grace. Such a conviction, however, is most often engendered and nourished in the Christian family, where both father and mother know, reverence and love the priesthood of Jesus Christ.

THE JURIDICAL MISSION
OF THE CHURCH

One of the paradoxes of the mystery of the Church is that, although she is, in her own right, a holy city (and indefectibly so), nevertheless the frontiers of this city of holiness will not be defined until one of the angels of the apocalypse measures it with a "golden reed," and finds it to be "four square," or perfect. (Cf. Ap 21,9–21.) This is to say that the Church exists in a period intermediate between Christ's ascension to the glory of his Father and his triumphant return on the Day of Judgment. This is to say also that the Church is endowed with a *mission*. She is, by definition, apostolic.[1]

---

[1] This is the fourth of the so-called "marks of the Church," which are contained in the creed recited at Mass. Our theological procedure, which is analytic, enables us to see these marks in their proper context. The Church's unity and catholicity were considered in connection with the distinction of members in the Church. Her holiness was seen to be based principally upon the continuation of Christ's priesthood. The

This mission, which we call juridical simply because it is based upon a divine command (cf. Mt 28,19f), is a rather complex thing. By way of introduction we shall discuss its complexity and then treat singly the elements of the mission itself.

First of all, we ought to understand that the mission of the Church is directed within as well as without. We may take the parish, the unit of the Church within the basic unit of the diocese, as an example. Within the territorial limits of an average parish members of the Church live as neighbors with those who are not incorporated into Christ's mystical body. Now, we may ask, if the Church as represented by this parish—its pastor and his assistants together with the people under their care—has a mission, to whom is it directed? The answer is, of course, that ideally the parish is always in a "state" of mission. Evidently there is a certain obligation on the parish to *go out* and make disciples of those who are not in the visible communion of the Church. It is also evident that all the members of the parish share this obligation somehow. To be Catholic is to be apostolic, missionary. The ways in which this mission can be exercised are countless. If we enlarge our view, we see that what is true of the parish is true of the Church as a whole. The most striking verification of this is the vast missionary effort conducted under the direction of the papal congregation of the Propagation of the Faith.

Turning back to the parish, however, we see that in its very inner constitution it has a missionary aspect. The pastor and his assistants have been *sent* to this particular locality to minister first of all to those who are "of the household of the faith." (Gal 6,10) They have been commissioned by the bishop of the diocese to share in his mission of feeding the flock that has been committed to his care. This commission is based on the recognition that this particular parish, as the entire

mark of apostolicity is, finally, to be understood in the present context of those principles which govern the Church's movement toward the goal established by Christ.

Were our procedure apologetic, the function of these four marks would be different. In that case, we should take each of them and show (1) that they must all be verified of the Church of Christ, and (2) that among all the societies which claim this title only the Roman Catholic Church can fully justify this claim. Such a procedure should lead to what the apologetes call a "judgment of credibility," that is, that it is reasonable to believe that the Roman Catholic Church is the Church of Christ. Such a judgment, however, is far from being an act of faith, because it is based on evidence collected by human reason.

The difference is vast. Here we are convinced by faith, that is, on the authority of God, that the Church is one, holy, catholic, and apostolic, and we are plumbing the meaning of this belief. It is a question of faith seeking understanding.

Church, is on the move. In this respect the Church is the fulfillment of the people of Israel who after having been led across the Red Sea out of Egypt go into the desert and begin a forty-year trek toward the promised land.

Beyond this twofold aspect of the Church's juridical mission, however, we must distinguish the *objects* of this mission. What is at stake here is perhaps even more important, for it is a question of discerning the very nature of the mission. In affirming that the mission of the Church is founded on a twofold power, namely to teach the truths of faith and to make and give sanction to laws, we are not disassociating the two powers in question. Doubtless they are connected most intimately; for this reason some theologians have preferred to consider them as one single power. (Cf. Charles Journet, *L'Église du Verbe Incarné*, I, 197ff.) Nevertheless, in the following pages we shall separate them and discuss how, in the Church, they are principles whereby her members, as well as those not yet incorporated, may be enlightened by divine truth and oriented toward the peace and tranquillity of the holy city.

Power to Teach

The Church moves toward her goal in faith and love. This is the principle of all that is left to be said about the powers of government at work in her. The first of them, the power infallibly to teach the Word of God, is for the engendering of the true faith in the souls of those to whom the gift of faith was communicated in the sacramental rite of baptism.

The meaning of the term, "the infallibility of the Church," is not always thoroughly understood. To make the meaning clear, we should say, first of all, that an infallible teaching authority is guaranteed by Christ, the author of the new creation, for the sake of the faith of the entire Church. Then, as to its nature, we should say that it is best defined as something negative. The very word indicates this. To be fallible is to be capable of error; to be *in*fallible is to be free from error.

A twofold question needs to be answered at this point: *what* are the data concerning which this gift of infallibility is to be exercised, and *who* in the Church is endowed with this gift? In other words, supposing that Christ is faithful to his promises to be with his Church to the end of time in this regard (cf. Mt 28,20) and to send another Paraclete to accomplish what he had established (cf. Jn 15,26; 16,13), what is the *object* of these promises, and who are the *subjects* endowed with this special assistance of infallibility?

First of all, the object of the Church's infallible teaching may be called the "deposit of faith." This deposit or body of truth, which, after a period of evolution (cf. S.Th., 2ᵃ 2ᵃᵉ,2,7–8), received its consummation in the Son of God, who was "appointed the heir of all things" (Heb 1,2), is contained in the holy Scriptures and sacred tradition.[2] These *data* constitute the rule which the Church herself is guided by in her teaching of the faith.

Finally, a word must be said about the *subject* of this infallible teaching power. Who in the Church is commissioned infallibly to teach the truths of the Catholic faith, and thus to constitute the principle by which the Church can "walk in faith" toward her goal?

Evidently the answer to these questions cannot be understood apart from what has been said in the chapter on distinction of office or function in the Church about the role of the hierarchy in transmitting divine things. The "teaching Church" is the hierarchy, that is, the college of bishops, the successors of the apostles, in union with and in subordination to the Roman pontiff.

Ordinarily, therefore, this infallible *magisterium* (teaching office) resides in the entire college of bishops as they propound the whole truth to the faithful committed to them, or to the world at large. This is, in fact, the meaning of the term, "ordinary *magisterium*."

In *extraordinary* circumstances, however, means are provided

---

[2] At present there is much discussion concerning the nature of this tradition. After long debates, the Council of Trent promulgated the following dogmatic formula: "All salutary truth and moral discipline . . . is contained in written books [that is, the Bible] and unwritten traditions, which were received by the apostles either from the very mouth of Christ or else from the inspiration of the Holy Ghost, and have come down to us, passed on, as it were, from hand to hand." (Cf. D783.) It is absolutely certain, therefore, that the end of the "time of revelation" coincides with the passing of the band of twelve whom Christ had chosen. The death of the last apostle is the end of the "fullness of time," if we take this phrase to mean the historical moment of the creation of the Church. What has been called into question is the sense of the disjunction made in this formula, "written books *and* unwritten traditions," since the expression was chosen both with the Protestant affirmation that the Scriptures are the sole rule of faith, and the variety of Catholic theories on the font(s) of revelation, clearly in mind. Did the conciliar fathers intend to define that there are some truths of Catholic faith which are not contained in the Scriptures *in some way*? This is a matter open to historical question and theological discussion.

75

whereby the sense of this *magisterium* can be determined more strikingly —even though these organs are by no means more infallible. First of all comes the Roman pontiff himself,

> when he speaks *ex cathedra,* that is, when, acting as the supreme pastor and teacher of all Christians, he defines with his supreme apostolic authority a doctrine of faith or morals to be held by the entire Church, in virtue of the divine assistance promised to him in the person of Peter, is vested with that infallibility with which the divine Redeemer willed his Church . . . to be endowed. (Vatican Council, Session IV [18 July, 1870], D1839)

We might note that this infallibility of the pope is but the epitome or classic instance of the infallibility of the Church. This is quite evident from the last phrase of the Vatican formula.

From this supreme function, the Roman pontiff, when speaking *ex cathedra,* derives the weight of his authority—when, for example, he writes an encyclical letter either to the entire Church, or else to some local church. Even the Holy Father does not bring to bear the full weight of his teaching authority in every case; still it may always be presumed that, when he exercises his teaching office, his expression of the truth is accurate with a "catholic" accuracy, and therefore has some universal application. Pope Pius XII points out, in one of his encyclicals, that such pronouncements are themselves a clear example of the *ordinary magisterium.* Therefore, they too call for the consent of the faithful. (*Humani Generis,* encyclical letter issued 12 August, 1950, par. 20. NCWC translation, p. 10)

A second extraordinary organ of the infallible magisterium is the ecumenical council, of which there have been twenty-one in the history of the Church. This institution has undergone much evolution in the course of the Church's existence. It can be defined as an assembly of the bishops of the Catholic Church which treats of questions of faith and the Church's life and organization, in union with and subordination to the head of the episcopal body and the teaching Church—the bishop of Rome. To him belongs the right to convoke, preside over, and close the council, as well as to confirm its results.

It can readily be seen that the ecumenical council is a striking symbol of the relation that exists at all times among the bishops, as well as between the episcopal college and the Roman pontiff. The relations are those established by Christ in the apostolic college itself, a fellowship of brothers bound together by their common union with and subordination to Peter, who was in total dependence upon Christ. Thus it is that the juridical mission in the Church to teach the faith is a collegiate affair; at its heart is the role of the brotherhood of bishops who share with Christ the office of mediating divine truth.

Power to Legislate

We have already said that St. Thomas's ideas concerning the new Law are likely to be used as a means to gain insight into the theology of the Church. Perhaps the most significant statement of all is that in which he makes the following distinction: (1) essentially the new Law of Christ is nothing less than the grace of the Holy Spirit (a fulfillment of the prophecy of Jeremia [31,33] and a favorite theme of St. Paul [e.g., Gal 5,13ff]); (2) even so,

> the new Law contains some things which are *dispositive* in relation to this grace, and which pertain to the use of it. These are, as it were, secondary elements of the new Law, concerning which Christ's faithful must be given direction, both in word and in writing. (*S.Th.*, 1ª 2ᵃᵉ,106,1)

It is entirely possible to see in this latter text a reference to the teaching of sacred truth. After all, the Church's magisterial function does dispose for the grace of faith. The truths of faith, moreover, are proposed in such a fashion as to demand assent. (Cf. Rom 1,5.)

Beyond this, however, there is another meaning which may be attached to the term, "secondary or dispositive elements of the new Law." We have said that the Church walks in faith and love; this means that there must be a power in the Church which disposes for the engendering of perfect love, as well as a power which guarantees the infallibility of her faith. This is the power in the Church to make, execute, and give sanction to "ecclesiastical laws."

It ought not to seem strange that this legislative power is conceived in relation to love. The function of any law (a reasonable disposition made by a superior in relation to the common good, and promulgated for his subjects), is to incline the subjects in question to be virtuous. In the Church, which has as its good the sanctity of perfect love, we

77

can see the quasi-necessity of moral direction given to the faithful in authoritative fashion. The laws of fast and abstinence, for example, are designed to give the Christian people the opportunity for the mortification of the senses which must be the mark of a disciple of Christ. Such self-denial, that is to say, the putting off of the "old man," is, of course, only the negative aspect of the Christ-life, and every such exercise is somehow ordained to the perfect work of charity in Christ's mystical body.

One other phrase in St. Thomas' remarks about the secondary elements of the new Law ought to be brought to bear here. He observes that they may pertain to the "use" of the grace of the Holy Spirit. We can see in this an allusion to all the law of the Church which is connected with the administration and the use of the sacraments. Thus those portions of the Church's Canon Law—the "sacred canons"—which are concerned with the making of laws (and not so much with the execution or sanction) are concerned with both "persons" and "things." Among these latter are the sacraments, sacred times and places, divine worship, and the temporal goods which are possessed by the Church.

This power is distributed in the Church in a manner analogous to the distribution of the power to teach. Significantly, the same Vatican Council which defined the infallibility of the pope, made the following dogmatic statement: ". . . by the institution of Christ, that is, by divine right, St. Peter has successors in perpetuity in the *primacy* over the universal Church; [and] the Roman Pontiff *is* St. Peter's successor in this respect." (Session IV [18 July, 1870], D1825) This is the authority for our saying that the jurisdiction to make laws for the entire Church, and for each one of her members, belongs to the Vicar of Christ, by virtue of his succession in the see of Peter. The biblical foundation for this jurisdiction is, again, the so-called "Petrine promises." (Mt 16,19) It is called a "primacy" because it is the principle or source of all other jurisdiction in the Church, and it is called universal, because it is not limited to any one part of the Church. It extends to the very limits of the visible and mystical body of Christ on earth.

Again, however, we should recall that St. Matthew records a similar saying of Christ made to the college of the apostles. (Mt 18,19) In fact, the words he uses in this second text are exactly the same, in reference to the power to "bind and loose." This is symbolic of a second aspect of the jurisdiction of the hierarchy in the Church. Each of the bishops who is possessed of a diocese, or who is the priest, teacher, and pastor of a local church, also claims a jurisdiction over his subjects which is of *divine* right, even though it is "particular." (Cf. decrees of the Vatican Council, Session IV [18 July, 1870], D1828.)

To join and balance the primacy of the Roman Pontiff and the particular jurisdiction of the local bishops may seem to be a delicate matter. The will of Christ is clear, however, and it is perfectly expressed in the words of Pope St. Gregory I:

> The honor due me is the honor due the entire Church. The honor given me is the solid strength of my brethren. And, in reality, I am then honored most when the honor due each and every one of them is not denied. (Letter to Eulogius, bishop of Alexandria, Book 8, ch. 30 [PL 77,933C])

A final word about the actual functioning of this canonical power of jurisdiction. We have said that it exists for the purpose of orienting all the members of the Church in the path of love. This is its remote purpose. More proximately, however, it is evident that this power to rule is meant to stabilize the historical existence of the Church, that is, under the light of the gospel or the New Law, to give the proper direction to the Church's march toward the New Jerusalem.

Normally this ecclesiastical discipline has to do with *exterior* acts, and it is limited to things which are of grave moment. Another delicate balance can be perceived here, namely, that there is no opposition between being "led by the Spirit" (cf. Gal 5,16ff) and faithful submission to the pastors of the Church. Once again appears clearly the nature of this mystery—an image of the incarnation of the Word of God, in the flesh of our own nature.

We have completed our brief and schematic study of the constitution of the Church. From first to last we have been conscious that divine Wisdom, in the person of Jesus Christ, is at work. This entire analysis was rooted in certain revealed figures of the mystery of a new creation, of which Christ is the author. Furthermore, even after having distilled from these figures an analogous concept of the Church's reality, we have been constrained, by the very nature of our task, to keep in constant contact with God's revealed Word, in order to understand the

79

mystery of membership and of the various offices in the Church. Finally, we have taken up the question of government, making use of the principle of mediation, and seeing how this principle is applied not only in the ministry of the Church's share in Christ's priesthood, but also in the transmission of truth and the conduct of ecclesiastical discipline. In so doing we have set the stage for a second part, in which we shall deal with the *activity* of the Church, under the sign of Love.

PART TWO

THE LOVE OF GOD
AND THE ACTION
OF THE CHURCH

The Church is catholic. In her the grace of Christ heals all wounds to make of mankind a new creation (top).

The Church is one. Everything in her proceeds from and returns to Christ (middle).

The Church is apostolic. The mission given by Christ to Peter and the other apostles is continued in her (left).

CHAPTER EIGHT

THE NEW JERUSALEM

There is no doubt but that the entire constitution of the Church, the new creation, is a work of divine wisdom, and, indeed, of Wisdom incarnate. This brief theology of the Church would be grossly incomplete, however, were we to content ourselves merely with this statement and an analysis of its implications. There remains to be considered the *activity* of this mystical person.

In order to understand the nature of this ecclesial activity, it is well to have in mind three aspects of Christ's fidelity to his spouse, the Church. First of all, he promised that, at the end of time, he would return to give her that joy and peace which are his by right. (Cf. Jn 14,18.28; 16,33.) Beyond that, however, he guaranteed that, notwithstanding the necessity of his ending the earthly sojourn during which he gave the Church her very being, he would really be *with* her to the end of time. (Cf. Mt 28,20.) Finally, our Lord indicated somewhat how this intermediate presence should be verified. "I will ask the Father and he will give you another Advocate to dwell with you forever, the Spirit of truth whom the world cannot receive, because it neither sees him or knows him. But you shall know him, because he will dwell with you, and be in you." (Jn 14,16f)

These promises dictate the order of what we must say about the Church's activity. The first of the three chapters in this concluding Part II will have as its subject that meeting with Christ to which the Church looks forward on the day of judgment. It is in the expectant hope of this encounter that the Church lives, day by day. Then we shall take up the questions of what the Church, as such, is doing "in the meantime." What is the activity most proper to her as the mystical spouse of Christ? What is the nature of her relations with other elements of creation, especially the political society?

Underlying all this, however, is the third aspect of Christ's fidelity to his Church. He is present with and in her *by his Spirit,* that other Advocate, whom he calls the "Spirit of truth." This is the key to the distinctive character of all ecclesial activity: it is "rooted and grounded in *love*." (Eph 3,18a) This is altogether true because the Holy Spirit, the soul of the Church, is the Spirit of love. Just as in the ineffable life of the blessed Trinity the Son of God proceeds from the Father as the Word, *Sapientia genita;* so the Spirit who comes from the Father and the Son *is* Love, *Amor procedens* (cf. S.Th., 1ª,37,1). Thus we see at the outset that in the following pages we shall be trying to clarify, in human language, the manner in which the mystery of the Church, as an image of the august mystery of the blessed Trinity, is consummated in love.

84 In beginning our discussion of the activity of the Church at a point which seems to be far removed from what we experience, namely, her heavenly state, we are guided by a fundamental principle in the tradition of Catholic theology. These chapters are, after all, in the realm of *moral* doctrine, the study of action ordered to an end. We begin, therefore, with the end, simply because it is regulative of everything which comes before. It is first in the order of intention. All our activity, as members of the Church, is ruled by our faith that *this* is the goal toward which we tend.

We must presuppose, in approaching this subject, the principles that are elaborated in any tract on beatitude. This means keeping in mind particularly that the happiness for which all men are destined by God—the salvation which he wills for all (cf. 1 Tim 2,4)—consists in the face to face vision of God, which is eternal life. (Cf. S.*Th.*, 1ª 2ᵃᵉ, 2,8; 3,8.) Our interest will be focused on the *ecclesial* aspects of beatitude. First of all, we shall point out the continuity of the Church's life on earth and that which she leads in heaven. Second, we shall discuss the most striking difference between the new paradise of heaven and the new creation, which is the Church on earth.

HOMOGENEITY OF THE CHURCH MILITANT AND THE CHURCH TRIUMPHANT

The terms used in the title of this section are familiar enough to preclude any lengthy explanation. We mean to say merely that the members of the Mystical Body of Christ, which, according to the teaching of Pius XII in *Mystici Corporis,* is identical with the one, holy, catholic, apostolic and Roman Church, are, as such, leading the same life—or acting in virtue of the same principles—as are the blessed in heaven. The Pope's consideration in the encyclical does not go beyond the limits of the Church militant. Thus, our use of the term, "Church," in reference to the blessed in heaven is an *extended* use. It does, however, have its roots in the tradition of the Church. The share of the life of God, of which the citizens of the new Jerusalem are possessed, is a face to face vision, for which their souls are elevated and strengthened by the "light of glory." (Cf. Ap 21,23 and S.*Th.*, 1ª,12,5.) The share in God's life, which is the lot of the members of the Church militant, is the knowledge and love of faith and charity for which their souls are elevated by the "light of grace." (Cf. Eph 5,8 and S.*Th.*, 1ª 2ᵃᵉ,110,2.)

Both, however, are real shares in the life of the blessed Trinity; this is the sense of the saying, "grace is the seed of glory." (Cf. 2 Pt 1,4.)

This is, no doubt, also the most fundamental sense of the term, the "communion of saints," which, in the Western form of the Apostolic Creed, follows immediately the phrase, "holy Catholic Church." (Cf. D6; also J. N. D. Kelly, *Early Christian Creeds,* pp. 388-97.) One of the greatest joys of Christian prayer is the loving contemplation of this communion, in which God distributes, with infinite largesse, his gifts to all the saints, and, at the same time, to those who are "called to be saints." (Cf. Rom 1,7; Eph 1,3–6.) But this is a prayer of faith!

THE HIERARCHY
OF THE NEW JERUSALEM

There is something entirely distinctive about the last two chapters of the Bible. (Ap 21–22) We should not be misled by the elaborate imagery employed here by St. John. After all, we have seen that the mystery of the Church is transmitted, first of all, in figurative ways. An attentive reading of this apocalyptic vision, "God's last word," as it were, will reveal to us what is distinctive about what he calls the new Jerusalem. (21,2)

Our discussion of the catholic unity of the Church revolved around two generic distinctions: (1) according to perfection; (2) according to office or function. The entire import of these last chapters of the Bible is that only one of these distinctions remains in the new Jerusalem or Church triumphant. The priestly hierarchy ceases to operate as mediator of divine gifts in the way that it did on earth. "I saw no temple therein," says St. John, "for the Lord almighty and the Lamb are the temple thereof. And the city has no need of the sun or the moon to shine upon it. For the glory of God lights it up, and the Lamb is the lamp thereof." (Ap 21,22f) The vision of each and every one of the saints is immediate; there is no mediation. (Cf. the apostolic constitution of Pope Benedict XII, *Benedictus Deus* [29 January, 1336] D530.) The only "hierarchy" of the new Jerusalem is one of perfection, with Christ consummately at the head of his bride, the Church.

86

> Then comes the end, when he delivers the kingdom to God the
> Father, when he does away with all sovereignty, authority, and power.

. . . And when all things are made subject to him, then the Son himself will also be subject to him who subjected all things to him, that God may be all in all. (1 Cor 15,24.28)

Among the mystical writers of Christian tradition, St. John of the Cross and St. Thérèse of Lisieux have both expressed this "hierarchy of perfection" through the figure of tumblers of different sizes, each filled to capacity, in order to indicate the perfect but diverse satisfaction of all human desires in the new Jerusalem. (Cf. St. John of the Cross, *Ascent of Mt. Carmel*, Book 2, ch. 5 [Garden City, N.Y.: Image, 1958], pp. 91-97.)

It is significant that in this last passage of Sacred Scripture, the mystical union of Christ with his Church is expressed through the image of the husband and the bride. This gives us an insight into the perfection of that figure; and it also suggests the sublimity of Christian marriage. (Cf. Eph 5,25–32.) Finally, it makes evident the authentic foundation of the so-called "mystical espousals" which some of the greatest saints of the church have experienced in their intimate relations with Christ.

And the Spirit and the bride say, "Come!" And let him who thirsts come; and he who wishes, let him receive the water of life freely. . . . "It is true, I come quickly!" Amen! Come, Lord Jesus! The grace of our Lord Jesus Christ be with all. Amen. (Ap 22,17.21)

CHAPTER NINE

ECCLESIAL ACTIVITY

If the new Jerusalem may fittingly be termed the Omega or conclusion of man's journey, then the next matter that requires consideration is the movement of the Church toward that Omega. It will be the final concern of this book.

ACTIVITY PROPER TO THE CHURCH

If a man is to act humanly, the activity must be at least under the command of reason. This is what it is to be a man: *esse secundum rationem,* in the language of the Schoolmen. In an analogous fashion, that mystical person which is the Church, if her activity is to be truly ecclesial, must act at the command of Christ, her head. Everything depends upon this: what does Christ ordain that his Church shall do?

The most obvious answer to this question is, of course, in the words of Christ himself: "Do *this* in remembrance of me!" (Lk 22,19b; cf. 1 Cor 11,24b) The eucharistic commemoration of Christ's Pasch is the activity of the Church *par excellence.* It is in this activity, in which she fulfills perfectly the command of Christ and is most intimately joined with him in holy communion, that she *is* most perfectly the Church. In the words of Pope Pius XII, "The mystery of the Most Holy Eucharist which Christ, the High Priest, instituted, and which he commands to be continually renewed in the Church by his ministers, is the culmination and the center, as it were, of the Christian religion." (*Mediator Dei,* Encyclical Letter of Pope Pius XII on the Sacred Liturgy, par. 66. NCWC translation, p. 27)

The study of the nature of the holy eucharist, precisely as a sacrifice offered by an ordained priest, and as a sacrament received by baptized communicants, belongs to sacramental theology. Therefore, our attention will be centered on only two aspects of this mystery: (1) the manner in which each and every one of the constitutional elements of the Church which we have analyzed in the first part of this volume is involved in this supreme ecclesial activity, and (2) the effect of this activity for the Church.

The eucharist has been celebrated in an almost infinite variety of circumstances—in the splendor of Roman basilicas, in plain rural parish churches, and in squalid prison camps. A striking illustration of this culminating activity is furnished when a bishop, surrounded by his priests and his people, offers this sacrifice in his church called a *cathedral,* because his chair is there. The bishop is, in the Church, the high priest; and this is why he is greeted at the door of his cathedral by the cry, *Ecce sacerdos magnus!*

First of all, then, in this eucharist celebration, Christ himself, the author of the new creation, is present. He is present in the person of the bishop, his representative; through the exercise of the bishop's priesthood, Christ deigns to become really present under the species of the bread and wine, which have been brought to the Church by the Christian people, as a symbol of all that they have and are.

The "Christian people," moreover, are there as members of the Church, exercising that share of the priesthood which is theirs in virtue of their embodiment in the Church through baptism. And to the degree that the people's share in this eucharistic celebration is active, that is, inasmuch as each of the *circumstantes* (those who stand around the altar) enters into the mystery of the Mass, to this degree is accomplished that Christian perfection which we spoke of as the term of incorporation into the mystical body of Christ. In other words, the individual growth of each Christian is measured in terms of his participation in a rite that is, of its very nature, the action of the Church as a community or communion.

The distinction, then, of hierarchy and laity is quite evident in the eucharist. "Divine things" are given and received according to the principle of mediation which Christ established in the new creation. His absolute supremacy is assured by his real presence, but he does not disdain sharing with his ministers the "dignity of causality."

Nor ought we to forget that even in the Mass—or, better, pre-eminently so—Christ is present as the Word of God. This celebration is, radically, a proclamation of God's Word and a response of his people. This is the place in which Christ manifests himself most of all as the "Word spirating Love" (S.Th., 1ᵃ,43,5, ad 2), because he gives *himself*. The sacrament of the body and blood of the Word made flesh, under the species of which he is really present, is a most perfect expression —a Word—in which God "speaks" his love to the Church.

In the eucharistic assembly, taken here as a striking example of the Church's activity, the effectiveness of Christ's government of the Church, in its twofold effect, is concretely expressed. In this Mass the Church is "on the move," and we can see how the bishop is, to one degree or another, achieving the ends of his juridical mission to teach and guide his flock. The passages from the sacred Scriptures which are appointed to be read—again, by ministers who belong in some way to the hierarchy —serve as the basis for a homily in which he propounds the gospel message in accord with the needs of these people, here and now. It will always be a question of both deepening the congregation's understanding of the truths of faith and directing them along the path of virtue. The reason for this is that the *kērygma*, which is the object of the preaching, though doubtless possessed of intellectual content, is known most perfectly only through action. To use the terms which we have employed in discussing juridical mission in the Church, the setting forth of the Word of God in these circumstances is, at least to some degree, an expression of the Church's ordinary *magisterium*. It is also a proposing of those secondary elements of the new Law which either dispose the Christian people for the grace of the Holy Spirit, or prepare them to use it well. (Cf. *S.Th.*, 1ª 2ᵃᵉ, 106,1.)

What, finally, is the effect of this ordered activity, this sacrifice, which is an efficacious proclaiming of God's Word and the response of his people? The answer to this question seems to be contained in an expression of the scholastics, as it is applied to the eucharist. It is said that the *res tantum* of this sacrament is the *unity of the Church*.[1] This means that as ecclesial activity *par excellence* the eucharist brings about that union of hearts which can only be accomplished in the catholic unity of the Church—union of the faithful in the heart of Christ, and their mutual love one for another. This *is* holy communion.

Thus, in the eucharist, the Church is not merely "on the move." She is also the image of that state in which "God is all in all." (1 Cor 15,28) Again, in the terms we have used in a previous chapter, it is above all in the eucharist that that good which is proper to her, the supernatural holiness of her members, is "conserved" and perfected, because this holiness consists in love. Holy communion, as we call it, is an intimate union of the Christian with Christ and through him with the other members of the mystical body, not to speak of the sublime intercourse of the soul with the persons of the blessed Trinity. These

---

[1] In all the sacraments St. Thomas distinguishes three things: *sacramentum tantum* (sign only), *res et sacramentum* (reality and sign), and the *res tantum* (reality only). The application of this distinction is most evident as regards those sacraments one of the effects of which is a spiritual *character,* for example, the character of baptism. In such a case, the *sacramentum tantum* is the external rite of baptism; the *res et sacramentum* (that which is at once reality effected by the external rite and a sacred symbol of something even more perfectly interior) is the character; finally, the *res tantum* is the grace proper to this sacrament, that is, the remission of all sin and incorporation into the body of Christ. This distinction is touched upon in the following texts: 3ª,63,3, ad 2 and 3ª,63,6, ad 3.

It is to be noted, moreover, that in applying the notion of *res tantum* to the eucharist, St. Thomas employs several different terms. (Cf. 3ª,73,1, arg. 2 and ad 3; art. 2, *sed contra;* art. 3; also 3ª,79,4.) Here we are using the term, "unity of the Church," because it seems to be a fitting translation of St. Thomas' *ecclesiastica unitas,* and also to translate well a longer phrase, in which he makes explicit reference to charity: "charity . . . not only with respect to its habitual practice but also as regards its act."

two aspects of holy communion correspond perfectly to the two elements of the single command to love God and, in him, our neighbor.

In using the example of the solemn celebration of the eucharist as the perfect expression of that activity which is most proper to the Church, we do not mean to imply that it is here alone that the fruits of the eucharist are obtainable in their fullness, nor that other eucharistic celebrations are the Church's activity in a less proper sense. Wherever the Mass is offered the whole Church acts, precisely because Christ, who bespeaks the whole Church, is the agent. All other activity, whether hierarchical or lay, is but a share in what he does.

In the life of most Catholics, the Sunday parish Mass is the place in which this communion is most of all to be accomplished. When the pastor of the parish gathers around himself the people who have been committed to him for the celebration of the eucharist, we have, as it were, a microcosm of the mystical body in which all the constitutive elements of the Church have their influence. One of the prime objectives of the liturgical renewal (or sacramental apostolate) is to give rebirth to the ecclesial sense of parish worship.

Putting the eucharist at the center of ecclesial activity is just another way of stating a principle laid down in sacramental theology: "All the other sacraments seem to be ordered to this sacrament as to their end." (*S.Th.*, 3ª,65,3) This is to say unequivocally that the other sacraments are also activities *in the Church,* in which her members are prepared in some way for the eucharist. And since the eucharist fulfills the perfection of charity in the Church, we may say that in a sense, it commands the other ecclesial actions, just as charity commands all the other virtues of the Christian life. Perfect eucharistic love requires that the members of the Church seek to sanctify their entire lives, and this principally through the sacraments. In other words, the use of the graces which belong properly to each of the sacraments is the normal means of Christian sanctification. This is also the source of the Church's missionary activity, which we have already discussed. The extension of the kingdom of Christ through the preaching of the Word, and the eventual establishing of the catechumenate, draws its inspiration and its power from that action of which the last words are: *Ite, missa est.*

To conceive of the activity of the Church as primarily eucharistic 92 is to suggest a rather important corollary for the moral life of the member of the Church. In the natural order it is true that there are some activities of man which are not the actions of the society of which he is a member —either familial or political. Thus the moral philosopher of old was justified in saying that there were three specifically distinct branches of his science: monastic, economic, and political. When, however, we take man as a member of that society which is Christ's mystical body, distinctions of this sort cease to have the same force. The most distinctive of his actions as a member is at once an action of the community of which he is a part. Thus, by extension, are verified the words of St. Paul: ". . . if one member suffers anything, all the members suffer with it, or if one member glories, all the members rejoice with it." (1 Cor 12,26)

THE CHURCH'S ACTIVITY
IN THE TEMPORAL ORDER

The Church is a new creation, but the "old" has not yet passed away. Nor does the Church so transcend the natural order that her life is lived in isolation from it. This fact is clear to all; it is the starting point of a whole ensemble of activities in which the Church enters into relation—and sometimes even conflict—with the "things of this world."

The first principle to be established in this context is that the Church is what is called a "perfect society." We have seen that the end which is established for her by Christ is altogether proper to her. We have already established what that end is, namely a supernatural one which absolutely transcends the natural order, and which is expressed concretely as the new Jerusalem. To affirm, however, that this is a perfect society means also that the Church is possessed of all the means necessary for the attainment of that end. This gives her a juridical freedom to seek that end without help or impediment from without.

Within the natural moral order, moreover, there are other societies, which may be either natural in the strict sense or "free," in the sense that they are constituted by man to attain some particular end. Examples of the first type of society are the family and political society; the second is exemplified by a corporation or a labor union. Among these the political society or state is alone "perfect." This means that only the political society is independent in seeking its own proper end, which is the

93

temporal welfare of all its citizens. Neither the family, even though it is the basic cell of all society, nor any of the "free" societies can claim this independence.

The question arises, therefore, of how the action and interplay of these various societies are related to the activity of the Church. It is a highly complex question. We can only hope to indicate its most fundamental aspects.

To begin from a negative point of view, it is evident that the Church has the absolute right not to be impeded in the fulfillment of her own mission. The gospel has a right to be preached. Preachers of the gospel have a right to be heard, wherever the circumstances permit their going. At some periods in the history of the Church, of course, she has been given positive help by the state in the exercise of this right. There does not seem to be any reason for which the Church should disdain such aid, as long as it does not jeopardize in any way the efficacy of her own action. We ought to be aware, however, of the long history of cesaro-papism, and the recurring necessity of the Church's claiming complete liberty even in her defense of spiritual values. She is not bound to any form of political society, either Western or Eastern, and is by very definition "extra-territorial." Her catholicity is not, in the first instance, geographical.

The positive aspect of the Church's contact with temporal society might be summed up in the term "illumination." The very subjects treated in some of the encyclicals of the modern popes suggest what is implied here: Leo XIII's *Immortale Dei* on the constitution of the Christian state, and his *Rerum Novarum* on the condition of labor; Pius XI's *Casti Connubii* on Christian marriage; John XXIII's *Mater et Magistra,* on more recent developments of the social question in the light of Christian teaching. Evidently the supernatural mission of the Church touches the temporal life of man by reason of what man is, a being whose destiny is not merely temporal, and the temporal good of whom is and must be subordinate to his supernatural end. Sometimes too the very content of temporal activity is subject to the illumination of the gospel, for example, when questions of the natural law are involved. Hence the insistence of the Church on the immorality of temporal systems which suppress the rights of the individual or of practices which are contrary to marriage even as an institution of nature.

94

This spiritual light which the Church can furnish temporal society seems to be concretized in two different spheres. First of all, in the sphere of Catholic Action, properly so-called, members of the Church enter into temporal society in order to offer it a leaven which is specifically Christian. Organizations such as the Young Christian Workers are pledged to preparing a Christian society, and to using means which belong to the Church as such, that is, cooperating with the hierarchy in its mission.

A second sphere of action, however, much broader in its implications, is that which might be called "profane" or cultural. Here all members of the Church are involved to the degree that they are members also of a given political or free society. Anything that a member of the Church can contribute to the commonweal of the family, political society, or "free" society to which he belongs may be looked upon as a remote preparation for the coming of the kingdom of Christ. Contributions to education, political action and cooperation, work and economic enterprises, ventures in the arts are, all human goods which, when seen in the light of the Catholic faith, become true goods, the promotion of which offers to the Church a milieu in which her mission can be carried on with greater efficacy.

Such a discussion, of course, would not be complete without some mention of the "problem of Church and state." Let it be said at the outset that no solution of the problem is to be offered, we shall merely attempt to outline the elements of the problem.

The vicissitudes of the relation between the Church and various states since the beginning of the Christian era might be put into two general categories—if we except that period in which the Church was "underground," that is, practically during the first three centuries of her life. (This situation reappears later, but has never affected the Church as a whole.) These categories are types of societies which have been called both sacral and pluralistic.

In the first of these two situations the rights of citizenship are accorded in a more or less strict dependence upon membership in the visible Church. Such a condition existed especially in medieval times. It appears that the doctrinal foundation for such an arrangement is the strict subordination of the natural to the supernatural. It is evident that such an organic relation of the Church and state could not possibly obtain except in a society in which all or the vast majority of men were or are Catholic.

The pluralistic arrangement is based upon other circumstances and other doctrinal considerations. First of all, the nations, or even localities, in the world where vast majorities of citizens are Catholic are relatively few. Besides, although always holding fast to the subordination mentioned above, it is true that the respective ends of the Church and political society are specifically distinct. This gives the political society a certain autonomy and provides the basis for an organization of it, in which the rights of citizenship are accorded to all, irrespective of their religious allegiance.

Such an arrangement does not necessarily mean an indifference toward religion on the part of the political society. In fact this is impossible, because of the natural obligations of the society, as well as the individuals who make it up, toward God. Nor does it mean, necessarily, complete "separation of Church and state," because the state is obliged, at the very least, to take away obstacles which may be present to its citizens from obtaining the legitimate fulfillment of their religious aspirations. It does involve, however, a certain "civil tolerance," in terms of which all the citizens are encouraged to seek a true relation with God. Such tolerance is not to be understood as a doctrinaire tolerance of error —or, what is worse, the promotion of error, which takes place in a society which is avowedly committed to an anti-God philosophy. It is rather a recognition that it is not, properly, within the competence of the political society, or of those who hold the authority within it, to "preach the gospel," that is, to seek the end which is proper to the Church.

The fact that the Church has existed—if not flourished—within the context of both types of society does not prove, of itself, that they are equally good. The judgments of what is ideal and what is to be sought here and now (which may be different, but not opposed in a contrary fashion) are to be made rather on the basis of two complementary principles: (1) the real subordination of the natural to the supernatural; (2) the real and specific distinction between these two orders. There is no doubt but that if the Church is given full freedom to act in accord with her constitution as the new creation, the political society in which she is implanted can only profit. The reason is that social justice, which is the commonweal of the political society, is perfected by the charity diffused through the Church's eucharistic activity.

CHAPTER TEN

SOURCES OF ECCLESIAL ACTIVITY

The natural movement of all contemplation is from understanding to love, from insight to delight. It is not strange, therefore, that, whereas the contemplation of the mystery of the Church begins with Christ, Wisdom incarnate, it ends with the Holy Spirit, the Spirit of love. The task of this last chapter is to consider how the Holy Spirit is at the heart of all the Church's activity.

97

THE HOLY SPIRIT:
SOUL OF THE CHURCH

At this point the process to be followed is quite obvious. To say that the Holy Spirit is the soul of the Church is, evidently, to have recourse to the Pauline formula—the Church is the body of Christ— and to apply to this figure a notion which is integral to it. St. Augustine witnesses to this tradition:

> In the Church, Christ's Body, the Holy Spirit plays the same role as the soul in the human body. Just as the soul acts in all the members of a single body, the Holy Spirit is active in the entire Church. (*Sermon* 267 [PL 38,1231]; cf. Pius XII, *Mystici Corporis*, par. 69; *op. cit.*, p. 31)

The real bases for making such a statement are indicated here and there in the works of St. Thomas. He points out, for example, that the entire supernatural life of man, which we would see as his life in the Church, is attributed to the Holy Spirit. The fundamental reason for this attribution is simply that the apex of this life is love, and the Holy Spirit is, in the mystery of the blessed Trinity the *nexus* of love between the Father and the Son. (Cf. S.C.G., 4,5,4; S.Th., 1ª,45,6, ad 2.) If we think of this life in terms of merit, again all the efficacy of man's cooperation with God is due to its "proceeding from the grace of the Holy Spirit." (S.Th., 1ª 2ᵃᵉ,114,3) Finally, the power of the sacraments themselves, which are in a sense constitutive of the Church, is based upon the power of the Holy Spirit. (Cf. S.Th., 3ª,66,9, quoting Jn 3,5.)

Trinitarian theology has something to offer here, by way of distinction. The work of sanctification is, in reality, a wonder for which God is responsible. It is attributed to one of the persons of the blessed Trinity because this is "appropriate." (On the principle of appropriation; cf. S.Th., 1ª,39,7. The essential attribute of God which is in question here is his holiness and love, as it is shared with man.) Everything which is an effect of love is attributed to the Holy Spirit because of the special character of his origin, to which we have already referred.

98   If, however, we are to exploit this figure of the Church's being *animated* by the Holy Spirit, we must think about it in terms of the functions of the soul. It is proper to a soul to be a principle of movement for the members of a body, and, more fundamentally, to dwell in that body. Evidently, it is necessary to observe the obvious canon in the use of symbolic language concerning divine things: the reality altogether transcends the symbol.

The movement of which we speak here is really everything that would possibly be included in the concept of "actual grace," that which St. Thomas calls "the divine help by which God moves us to will the good and to do it." (*S.Th.*, 1ª 2ªᵉ,111,2) This action of the Holy Spirit extends to the very limits of what we know to be the Church, even though our perception of these limits must be imperfect. Where grace inspires men to know God and to do his will, there the Holy Spirit is at work. And because he is the Spirit of Christ, there, too, in some sense, the Church is being perfected in her catholic unity. Most of all, however, the actual graces which have their origin in the use of the sacraments, especially the eucharist, are "movements" due to the Holy Spirit as soul of the Church. This is so true that the most precious of graces, those which belong to heroic sanctity, are called in Christian tradition operations of the "gifts of the Holy Spirit." (Cf. *S.Th.*, 1ª 2ªᵉ, 68,1–5.)

To say that the Holy Spirit dwells in the Church, moreover, is a statement based upon the most sublime mystery of Catholic spirituality: the indwelling of the Holy Spirit in the souls of the just. Pope Pius XII indicates somewhat the limits of what must be our groping to understand this doctrine, and at the same time puts us on guard, by intimating that this indwelling presence in the Church by the Holy Spirit cannot possibly be conceived as an "embodying" of what is properly divine in the creature.

> Let all agree uncompromisingly . . . to reject every kind of mystic union by which the faithful would in any way pass beyond the sphere of creatures and rashly enter the divine, even to the extent of one single attribute of the eternal Godhead being predicated of them as their own. (*Mystici Corporis*, par. 94; *op. cit.*, p. 39)

Another profound mystery remains still to be fathomed.

Meditation on this truth must begin from a common principle, namely, God's presence in all things he has created and continues to maintain in existence, according to his "immensity." (Cf. *S.Th.*, 1ª,8,1 and 3.) With this as a starting point, we ask what is peculiar about the presence of God in the souls of the just, that is, those members of the Church who are in living union with Christ? This presence is called an "indwelling presence"; but what does this mean? St. Thomas answers this question quite simply:

> There is a special [mode of the divine presence] which belongs to the rational creature, according to which God is said to be present as the thing known is in the knower and the beloved is present to the lover. Because, moreover, in knowledge and love, the rational creature attains God himself, in this special way God is said not merely to be present to him, but even to dwell in him as in his temple. (*S.Th.*, 1ª, 43,3)

In this way, then, God is the soul of our soul, insofar as through the medium of sanctifying grace, an "habitual gift divinely infused in our souls" (*S.Th.*, 1ª 2ªᵉ,111,2), the divine persons come to be our guests, even to be "possessed" by us. This special presence, the delight of all the saints, presupposes the presence of God, by his "immensity," but it is altogether distinct from it because it is supernatural.

From this truth to that according to which the Holy Spirit is the indwelling soul of the Church, Christ's mystical body, is but one step, because we can see that this soul is wholly in every member; concomitantly his presence in the Church is undivided. We should understand that while this is theology and not faith, it is still according to the mind of St. Paul. (Cf. 1 Cor 3,16; 6,19.)

The soul of the Church, then, is uncreated; his presence and impulse in the Church are her very life-breath. Furthermore this presence and impulse are diffused in the Church through created gifts such as we have already mentioned: sanctifying and actual grace. Even these gifts, the proximate principles of all ecclesial activity, are composite. We are referring especially to the theological virtues of faith, hope, and charity, which are the "soul" of the interior life. The work of these virtues is most evident in the activity of the Church most proper to her —eucharistic worship. These are all armatures, as it were, of the informing and dynamic presence of the Holy Spirit in the Church.

THE CHURCH AS OUR MOTHER

These considerations open up for us another aspect of the intercourse of activity within the Church, especially as regards the relations existing between the hierarchy and the laity. The hierarchical functions, participations in the powers of Christ as prophet, priest, and king, are in reality so many gifts of the Holy Spirit. Their special character is at the very least suggested by St. Paul in the first epistle to the Corinthians. (12,28ff) These gifts are not communicated solely for the growth in holiness of the individual, but are also given for the building up of the Church. (Cf. *S.Th.*, 1ª 2ᵃᵉ,111,1,4–5.)

Their exercise is, furthermore, maternal, to use a figure that is familiar to Catholic tradition. The Church is our mother. In sacramental worship, in the transmission of truth, and in the application of the "holy canons" the Church has guided us as a mother directs her children, enlightening them and putting them on the path of virtue. In this role the hierarchy itself depends upon the Holy Spirit and his charisms.

If this be true of the hierarchy, however, it is certainly all the more true—though in a vastly different way—of our Lady. At the time of the annunciation, the angel said to her: "The Holy Spirit shall come upon you and the power of the Most High shall overshadow you." (Lk 1,35a) The fulfillment of this prophecy, of course, consists first of all in the mystery of the incarnation, in which he was conceived who was from eternity "begotten Wisdom," and who from the first moment of his human life was the head and author of the New Creature. We cannot, however, separate this mystery of our Lady's divine maternity from the mystery of her spiritual maternity with respect to the members of the mystical body of her Son. In fact the latter flows from the former in virtue of our Lady's *fiat,* because in this assent she opened her heart to the will of God for her in the mystery of the *redemptive* incarnation. She was to be not merely the vessel through which is communicated to mankind him who is "full of grace and truth." (Jn 1,14) She is also the Woman, type and figure of the Church, through whom is verified that affirmation of the beloved disciple, given to her as her cherished son at the foot of the cross: "of his fullness we have all received, grace for grace." (Jn 1,17)

Our own grasp of the truths that the Holy Spirit is the very life, breath, and soul of the Church, and that, for this very reason, the Church is our mother, is dependent in great measure on our understanding of our Lady's share in the gifts of the Holy Spirit. All of her privileges have an ecclesial sense; above all her vocation to be the mother of the divine Redeemer, as well as all those graces which prepared her for this role, manifest the same. Her immaculate conception and perfect sinlessness are the very type of the Church's vocation to be "without spot or wrinkle or any such thing . . . holy and without blemish." (Eph 5,27) Her perpetual virginity is the perfect realization of the mystery of the Church's virginal espousals, as a chaste bride, to Christ. (Cf. 2 Cor 11,2.) Her assumption is, together with the ascension of our Lord, the source of the Church's hope and expectation that St. John's prophecy will be fulfilled in us: "And I saw the holy city, New Jerusalem, coming down out of heaven from God, made ready as a bride adorned for her husband. And I heard a loud voice from the throne saying, 'Behold the dwelling of God with men, and he will dwell with them. And they will be his people, and God himself will be with them as their God." (Ap 21,2f)

Suggested Readings

CHAPTER ONE

Sacred Scripture
Col 1,13-20
Eph 1,3-23

Congar, Y. M.-J., "The Idea of the Church in St. Thomas Aquinas," and "The Mystical Body of Christ," in *The Mystery of the Church* tr. A. V. Littledale (Baltimore: Helicon, 1960), 97-137. Cf. *The Thomist*, 1 (1939), 331-59 for the scholarly apparatus of the first of these essays.

Dublanchy, E., "L'Église," in *Dictionnaire de Théologie Catholique*, t. 4, p. 2, 2108-24.

Lubac, H. de, "The Church as Mystery," in *The Splendour of the Church* tr. M. Mason (New York: Sheed and Ward, 1956), pp. 1-28.

Pius XII, *Mystici Corporis* (*The Mystical Body of Christ*), 3d ed.; introduction and notes by J. Bluett (New York: America Press, 1957), par. 42-44, 22f; par. 58-64, 27ff. For authentic text of this encyclical, see also *AAS*, 35 (1943), 193-248.

St. Thomas Aquinas, *Summa Theologiae*, 3,7-8.

CHAPTER TWO

Sacred Scripture
Ac 2,1-11
1 Cor 11,23-26
2 Cor 5,16-19
Gn 1-2
Mt 16,13-20; 18,15-18; 26,26-29; 28,16-20
Jn 1,1-18; 19,31-34

Congar, Y. M.-J., *Christ, Our Lady, and the Church*, tr. H. St. John (Westminster, Md.: Newman, 1956).

————, "The Church and Pentecost," in *The Mystery of the Church*, 1-57.

Journet, C., "L'Église, Prémices de l'Univers Rassemblé dans le Christ," *L'Église du Verbe Incarné*, Vol. II (Paris: Desclée de Brouwer, 1951), 97-186; and "La Vierge est au coeur de l'Église," *ibid.*, 382-453.

Lubac, H. de, "The Church and Our Lady," in *The Splendour of the Church*, 238-89.

Pius XII, *Mystici Corporis*, par. 32-41 (*op. cit.*, pp. 19-22); par. 130 (*op. cit.*, 51-52).

St. Thomas Aquinas, *Summa Theologiae*, 3,48-49.

CHAPTER THREE

Sacred Scripture
  1 Cor 12,12-30
  Eph 2,19-22; 5,21-32
  Jn 15,1-17
  Mt 13,1-52
  Rom 12,4-8

Cerfaux, L., *The Church in the Theology of St. Paul* (New York: Herder and Herder, 1959).

Congar, Y. M-J., "Lectio Divina," in *Le Mystère du Temple*, 22 (Paris: Éditions du Cerf, 1958), 188-205; Eng. tr. *The Mystery of the Temple* (Baltimore: Helicon, 1962).

Lubac, H. de, "The Two Aspects of the One Church," in *The Splendour of the Church*, 55-86.

Mersch, E., S.J., *The Theology of the Mystical Body*, tr. C. Vollert (St. Louis: B. Herder, 1951).

Pius XII, *Mystici Corporis*, par. 15-28 (*op. cit.*, pp. 15-18); par. 73-99 (*op. cit.*, 32-44).

CHAPTER FOUR

Bea, Augustin Cardinal, "The Position of Catholics Regarding Church Unity," in *The Ecumenical Council and the Laity* (New York: Paulist Press, 1962), pp. 3-23.

Congar, Y. M.-J., *Chrétiens Désunis*, "Unam Sanctam," 1 (Paris: Éditions du Cerf, 1937) (Eng. tr., *Divided Christendom* [London: Geoffrey Bles, 1939]).

Hamer, J., "Place des religieux dans l'apostolat de l'Église," in *Nouvelle Revue Théologique*, 81 (1959), 271-81.

Leeming, B., *The Churches and the Church, A Study of Ecumenism.* (Westminster, Md.: Newman Press, 1960).

Liégé, A., "L'appartenance à l'Église et l'encyclique *Mystici Corporis*," in *Revue de Sciences Philosophiques et Théologiques*, 32 (1948), 351-58.

Lumière et Vie, 18 (1954). [Several articles on the axiom, *Extra ecclesiam. . . .*]

Journet, C., *L'Église du Verbe Incarné,* Vol. II, 1027-1114 ("Qui est Membre du Christ et de l'Église," and " 'Hors de l'Église pas de Salut.' ")

Pius XII, *Mystici Corporis,* par. 29-31 (*op. cit.,* pp. 18-19).

Rahner, K., "Die Zugehörigkeit zur Kirche nach der Lehre der Enzyclik Pius XII," in *Zeitschrift für Katholische Theologie,* 69 (1947), 129-88.

St. John, H., "Our Separated Brethren," *Worship,* 37:1 (Dec., 1962), 74-83.

St. Thomas, *Summa Theologiae,* 2ª 2ªᵉ,184; 3ª,69,4.

CHAPTER FIVE

Sacred Scripture
Eph 4,7-16

Congar, Y. M.-J., "The Church and its Unity," in *The Mystery of the Church,* 58-96.

————, *Lay People in the Church,* tr. D. Attwater (Westminster, Md.: Newman, 1959).

————, "Structure du sacerdoce chrétien," in *La Maison-Dieu,* 27 (1951), 51-85.

Journet, C., *L'Église du Verbe Incarné,* Vol. I, 989-1026.

Lécuyer, J., "Essai sur le sacerdoce des fidèles chez les pères," in *La Maison-Dieu,* 27 (1951), 7-50.

Palmer, P., "Lay Priesthood—Real or Metaphorical?" *Theological Studies,* 8 (1947), 574-613; "The Lay Priesthood—Towards a Terminology," *Ibid.,* 10 (1949), 235-50.

Rea, J. E., *Common Priesthood of the Members of the Mystical Body of Christ* (Washington, D.C.: The Catholic University of America Press, 1947).

St. Thomas Aquinas, *Summa Theologiae,* 3ª,63.

CHAPTER SIX

Sacred Scripture
Heb 8

Pius XII, *Mystici Corporis,* par. 45-57 (op. cit., pp. 23-26).

St. Thomas Aquinas, *Summa Theologiae,* 1ª,22,3; 3ª,26.

CHAPTER SEVEN

Jedin, H., *Ecumenical Councils in the Catholic Church* (New York: Herder and Herder, 1950).

Journet, C., *L'Église du Verbe Incarné*, Vol. I (Paris: Desclée de Brouwer, 1955). (This volume is translated as *The Church of the Word Incarnate*, [New York: Sheed and Ward, 1955].)

d'Ormesson, W., *The Papacy*, 81 in "Twentieth Century Encyclopedia of Catholicism" (New York: Hawthorn, 1959).

St. Thomas Aquinas, *Summa Theologiae*, 3ª,22.

CHAPTER EIGHT

Sacred Scripture
   Ap 19,11-22,21.

Journet, C., *L'Église*, Vol. I, 20-23 ("Le Régime futur de l'Église").

CHAPTER NINE

Foster, P., *Two Cities, A Study of the Church-State Conflict* (Westminster, Md.: Newman, 1955).

Journet, C., *L'Église*, Vol. I (on Church and State), 246-425; Vol. II (on the mission of the Church), 1223-52.

Jungmann, J. A., *Public Worship* (Collegeville, Minn.: The Liturgical Press, 1957).

Lubac, H. de, "The Church in the World," in *The Splendour of the Church*, 114-46.

Miller, J., "The Nature and Definition of the Liturgy," *Theological Studies*, 18 (1957), 325-56.

Murray, J. C., *We Hold These Truths* (New York: Sheed and Ward, 1960).

Pius XII, *Mediator Dei*, Encyclical letter on the Sacred Liturgy (Washington, D.C.: NCWC, 1948).

CHAPTER TEN

Sacred Scripture
   I Cor 3,16f; 6,19
   Jn 14,16f.25f; 16,12f.
   Rom 5,1-5.

Journet, C., *L'Église*, Vol. II, 522-580 (on the "uncreated" and "created" souls of the Church).

Lubac, H. de, "Ecclesia Mater," in *The Splendour of the Church*, 174-207.

Mura, E., "L'âme du Corps mystique. Est-ce le Saint-Esprit ou la grâce sanctifiante?" *Revue Thomiste* (1936), 233-52.

Pius XII, *Mystici Corporis*, par. 65-72 (op. cit., pp. 29-32); par. 107-23 (*op. cit.*, pp. 43-49).

ABBREVIATIONS

The Books of the Old and New Testaments

Genesis	Gn	Canticle of Canticles	Ct
Exodus	Ex	Wisdom	Wis
Leviticus	Lv	Sirach (Ecclesiasticus)	Sir
Numbers	Nm	Isaia	Is
Deuteronomy	Dt	Jeremia	Jer
Joshua	Jos	Lamentations	Lam
Judges	Jgs	Baruch	Bar
Ruth	Ru	Ezechiel	Ez
1 Samuel (1 Kings)	1 Sm	Daniel	Dn
2 Samuel (2 Kings)	2 Sm	Osea	Os
1 Kings (3 Kings)	1 Kgs	Joel	Jl
2 Kings (4 Kings)	2 Kgs	Amos	Am
1 Chronicles (Paralipomenon)	1 Chr	Abdia	Abd
2 Chronicles (Paralipomenon)	2 Chr	Jona	Jon
Ezra	Ez	Michea	Mi
Nehemia (2 Ezra)	Neh	Nahum	Na
Tobia	Tb	Habacuc	Hb
Judith	Jdt	Sophonia	So
Esther	Est	Aggai	Ag
Job	Jb	Zacharia	Za
Psalms	Ps(s)	Malachia	Mal
Proverbs	Prv	1 Machabees	1 Mc
Coheleth (Ecclesiastes)	Coh	2 Machabees	2 Mc

In the enumeration of the Psalms, the first number follows the Vulgate, the number within brackets, the Hebrew text.

St. Matthew	Mt	1 Timothy	1 Tim
St. Mark	Mk	2 Timothy	2 Tim
St. Luke	Lk	Titus	Ti
St. John	Jn	Philemon	Phlm
Acts of the Apostles	Ac	Hebrews	Heb
Romans	Rom	St. James	Jas
1 Corinthians	1 Cor	1 St. Peter	1 Pt
2 Corinthians	2 Cor	2 St. Peter	2 Pt
Galatians	Gal	1 St. John	1 Jn
Ephesians	Eph	2 St. John	2 Jn
Philippians	Phil	3 St. John	3 Jn
Colossians	Col	St. Jude	Jude
1 Thessalonians	1 Thes	Apocalypse	Ap
2 Thessalonians	2 Thes		

Apocrypha and Qumrân Material

Henoch	Hen	Testament of the	
Jubilees	Jub	Twelve Patriarchs	Test
Psalms of Solomon	Ps Sol	Manual of Discipline	MD

Other Source Material

Acta Apostolicae Sedis
  [Acts of the Apostolic See] AAS
Ancient Christian Writers,
  ed. J. Quasten and others ACW
Acta Sanctae Sedis
  [Acts of the Holy See] ASS
Codex Iuris Canonici
  [Code of Canon Law] CIC
Denzinger-Bannwart, Enchiridion
  Symbolorum, 30th ed. [Handbook
  of the Creeds] D
Patrologia, series graeca,
  ed. J. P. Migne PG
Sacrorum Conciliorum nova
  . . . Collectio Mansi

Patrologia, series latina,
  ed. J. P. Migne PL
Summa contra Gentes
  S. Thomae Aquinatis S.C.G.
Quatuor Libri Sententiarum
  Petri Lombardi [Four Books
  of Opinions] Sent.
Summa Theologiae
  S. Thomae Aquinatis S.Th.
Supplementum tertiae partis Summae
  Theologiae (Ottawa ed. 1941)
  Suppl.
The Church Teaches,
  ed. J. Clarkson and others TCT

INDEX